THE
KING OF LOVE

Meditations on the Twenty Third Psalm

J. D. JONES

AMBASSADOR
BELFAST ◆ **GREENVILLE**
NORTHERN IRELAND ◆ SOUTH CAROLINA

The King Of Love

First published 1922
This edition 1998

ISBN 1 84030 035 3

Ambassador Publications
a division of
AMBASSADOR PUBLICATIONS LTD
Providence House
16 Hillview Avenue,
Belfast, BT5 6JR
Northern Ireland

Emerald House
1 Chick Springs Road, Suite 203
Greenville,
South Carolina 29609, USA
www.emeraldhouse.com

THE KING OF LOVE

The Twenty Third Psalme

THE LORD is my shepheard,
I shall not want.
He maketh me to lie downe in
greene pastures. He leadeth mee beside the still waters.
He restoreth my soule. He leadeth
me in the pathes of righteousnes,
for His name's sake.
Yea though I walke through the valley
of the shadowe of death, I will feare
no evill. for Thou art with me, Thy
rod and Thy staffe, they comfort me.
Thou preparest a table before me, in
the presence of mine enemies. Thou
anointest my head with oyle, my cuppe
runneth over.
Surely goodnes and mercie shall
followe me all the daies of my life.
and I will dwell in the house of
the LORD for ever.

Authorized-King James-Version of 1611

Contents

7

CONTENTS

I

THE SHEPHERD PSALM

The King of Love my Shepherd is,
　Whose goodness faileth never;
I nothing lack if I am His
　And He is mine for ever.

Where streams of living water flow
　My ransomed soul He leadeth,
And, where the verdant pastures grow,
　With food celestial feedeth.

Perverse and foolish oft I strayed,
　But yet in love He sought me,
And on His shoulder gently laid,
　And home, rejoicing, brought me.

In death's dark vale I fear no ill
　With thee, dear Lord, beside me;
Thy rod and staff they comfort still,
　Thy cross before to guide me.

Thou spread'st a table in my sight;
　Thy unction grace bestoweth,
And O what transport of delight
　From Thy pure chalice floweth.

And so through all the length of days
　Thy goodness faileth never:
Good Shepherd, may I sing Thy praise
　Within Thy house for ever.

—Sir H. W. Baker.

THE SHEPHERD PSALM

THE SHEPHERD

FOR many and various reasons a preacher rather shrinks from making this short but most exquisite of Psalms his theme. To begin with, there is the familiarity of the Psalm itself. It is easier far to speak or write upon an unfamiliar passage than upon one whose every word by constant and repeated usage has become familiar and dear. And more familiar verses than those of this Psalm the Bible does not contain. People have meditated so often and so deeply upon the words of this Psalm, and so much has been said and written about it that one is naturally inclined to think that everything that can be profitably said about it has already been said, that all the truth it contains has been discovered, that its very last drop of sweetness has been extracted, and that therefore any preacher or writer who should venture to make the verses of this Psalm his theme would be but repeating a thrice-told tale.

Further, this little Psalm is not only the most familiar of the Psalms, it is also the most sacred and dear. It comes to us burdened with all sorts of hallowed associations. In its words men and women all down the centuries have given expression to their faith and hope. It is the Psalm with whose words they have sustained themselves in life's great hours.

This is the Psalm which Augustine calls the "martyr's Psalm," because it was with its words upon their lips that the Christians of the early days faced the lions and the sword and the fire. This was the Psalm with which Luther comforted his soul in a time of sore sickness. This was the Psalm which Isabel Alison and Marion Howie sang as they were taken to the scaffold at Edinburgh. "Come, Isabel," said Marion Howie—and she was but twenty years of age—"let us sing the Twenty-third Psalm "—and so together they went down into the valley singing in the glad assurance that God was with them. It was with this Psalm on their lips or in their ears that men as different as Archbishop Laud, Edward Irving —that great but erratic religious genius—and Dr. Duff, the great Indian missionary, faced their end. And for most of us it has not historical associations simply, but personal associations, too. This is a Psalm which was specially dear to our own loved and lost. This is the Psalm with whose great declaration of the Shepherd's love and care they comforted themselves as they drew near to the valley. This is the Psalm which has brought balm and healing to our own hearts as we have been gathered round the open grave. Now it seems almost an irreverent thing to examine and analyze, to discuss and criticize a Psalm that occupies so unique a place in the affections of men as this Psalm does. It is like criticizing your mother's face. The fitting thing seems to be to let the Psalm do its own work, and make its own impression, and convey its own spirit of quiet and happy trust to the heart.

And then there is always the risk of marring the perfect beauty of the Psalm by careless handling. The exquisite bloom of the flower is soon spoiled if you begin to handle it. I suppose the work of the botanist is useful and necessary; I suppose it is just as well we should know all about the structure of the flowers— but oftentimes as the botanist examines the structure of the flower its beauty gets disfigured, if not totally destroyed. And the preacher who weighs and examines every word is much like the botanist. He may destroy the beauty of a Psalm like this—rob it of its bloom —in the very effort to explain it. He may make people wish that he would leave them alone to enjoy the beauty of the flower, instead of insisting upon dissecting it. And the fear of doing that is enough to make any one shrink. Better let the flower bloom there in its own native and unmistakable beauty than run the risk of spoiling it by rough handling. All these considerations have had their weight with me. Nevertheless, I am going to venture to speak about these familiar verses—with the hope in me that I may be kept from saying anything that shall mar their beauty, but that God will use me to bring out of them things new as well as things old for the profit of you who read. I am going to study these sacred verses in the hope that as we look steadily into them we may discover depths of tenderness in them which shall make them more sacred still. I am going to speak about this exquisitely beautiful little Psalm in the hope and with the prayer that as the result of patient examination it may shine for us with a beauty more transcendent yet.

THE AUTHOR OF THE PSALM

This first study shall be mainly by way of introduction. To begin with, I want to say a word or two about the authorship of the Psalm. It is in the minds of ordinary Christian people inseparably associated with the name of David.

That is what the title calls it: "A Psalm of David." It is only fair, however, to say that the titles of the Psalms, while undoubtedly ancient, were added later than the date of the Psalms themselves and are therefore not absolutely sure and reliable evidences of authorship. They tell us who were traditionally supposed to be the authors of the Psalms in question. But their witness is by no means unimpeachable. There are numbers of Psalms whose titles are quite obviously wrong. The statement of the title is refuted oftentimes by the contents of the Psalm. The critics have been, as you know, busy with the book of Psalms, as they have been with the other books of the Old Testament, and as a result of their investigations they have been led to assign to other hands and to a much later date many of the Psalms which by their titles are attributed to David. With many of their judgments honest students are simply bound to agree. We may not like to have our traditional ideas upset, and it goes against the grain perhaps to have to assign to some unknown author of quite late date Psalms which we had always identified with the romantic figure of David the shepherd king—but I want to insist upon it that the religious value of a Psalm in no way depends upon any question of its authorship or date.

I would not say that questions of date and authorship do not affect the value of historic books like the Gospels and the book of the Acts. Quite obviously they do. We should have less confidence in the historic accuracy of the events they narrate if it could be proven that the Gospels themselves were late productions. But in a purely religious book such as the book of Psalms, questions of date or authorship scarcely count. I think Christian people have often given themselves quite needless trouble by imagining that these literary questions which scholars have been for the past fifty years or more discussing somehow or other menaced the truth of the inspiration of the Bible. A moment's thought, however, will show that they do not and can not. It would do us a world of good to get hold of a simple truth like this—a passage of Scripture is inspired not because a certain man wrote it, but *because God speaks through it*. That is really what inspiration means—or rather that is what we mean when we say a verse, a paragraph, a book is inspired—we mean that in it and through it we can hear the voice of God. The value of a verse of Scripture, therefore, does not at all consist in the fact that David or Isaiah wrote it, but in the fact that it conveys religious truth and that through it God speaks to the soul. And therefore this follows—and this is the point I want to get home—if through a passage of Scripture God plainly speaks to the soul, it does not cease to be inspired even though it should be proved that neither David nor Isaiah wrote it, but some saint of God whose name has perished out of memory. I will venture to say that in actual practice we recognize the truth of all this, for when we read the great words of Scripture—its assertions about God, its glowing promises, its mighty words of inspiration, its splendid anticipations of the future—we never trouble our heads as to who wrote them. What matters who the human mouthpiece may have been, if we hear the voice of God in them. So it would not disturb me very much, nor would it— for me—in the slightest degree detract from the spiritual value of this Psalm, if the critics should be able to demonstrate that it was not written by David after all. There are some who take that position, as you know. They say that the Psalmist here is not really speaking in his own name—he is speaking in the name of the nation. It is Israel—speaking through the Psalmist—who says " the Lord is my shepherd." And they go on to say that such a Psalm as this, so full of serene and quiet confidence, could never have been written in the time of a nation's youth. " A long experience," they say, " of need and trouble, as well as of comfort and help, lies behind this Psalm."

Now all this seems to me a case of the over-refinement of criticism. This habit of depersonalizing Scripture and of regarding individual assertions as made—not of the individual, as the plain sense of the passage would suggest, but of the community—has become a craze with some critics. One has only to read this little Psalm to feel that it is far too intimate and personal to be referred to the nation of Israel. Such an idea takes all the pith and glow and warmth out of the Psalm. It is not a community that speaks here, but an individual pouring out his own trust and confidence in God. And as for their assertion that a great deal of need and trouble, as well as of comfort and help, lie behind this Psalm, they forget that all the experience of need and trouble, of comfort and help, which the Psalm demands can be compassed within the limits of a single life. I agree that this is not a Psalm of youth, it is a Psalm of experienced manhood, if not of age. But the plain and obvious account of the Psalm is, I am persuaded, in this case the true account—this is the outpouring of the heart of a man who has had his share of trial and trouble, but who has found that the Lord keeps him from all harm. And in all the history of Israel I know of no individual from whose lips and from whose heart this Psalm is more likely to have come than from the shepherd king to whom the title assigns it. So—although I repeat that the spiritual value of the Psalm would be in no way impaired should the title by further research be proved to be incorrect—I am going, in my exposition of the Psalm, to take it for granted that it is in very deed a Psalm of David. But of David in his old age. David in his youth could not have sung this Psalm. He had to pass through these vicissitudes, of which his career was full, before he could indite this Psalm. Which of our own poets is it that says:

> " Most wretched men
> Are cradled into poetry by wrong;
> They learn by suffering what they teach in song " ?

There is a bitter tang about that couplet, but there is a truth in it: men have to experience life before they can really speak about it. And David had to experience danger and trouble before he could speak of God's keeping care. The David who wrote this Psalm was not the care-free shepherd lad of Bethlehem, but the David who had been a hunted outlaw, the David who had been relentlessly pursued by the murderous wrath of King Saul, the David against whom his son Absalom had rebelled, and who had seen his kingdom fall away from him, the David who in the course of life had been led into many a valley of deep gloom, but who nevertheless ended his days in honour and quietness and peace. And it adds enormously to the comforting power of the Psalm that it is such a man who sings it. This is not the bright but baseless optimism of youth. This is not the cheerfulness of the untried. This is the testimony of a man who has been through the fire; this is the witness of a man who has struggled in the floods of deep waters. This man speaks what he knows and testifies what he has seen. He has faced life's difficulties, its disappointments, its crushing sorrows, and this is his resulting testimony that God has been to him so kind and faithful a shepherd, that he has absolutely no fear as to what coming days may bring. His temper is one of serene and happy trust. "The Lord is my shepherd, I shall not want."

GOD—THE SHEPHERD

This image of the "shepherd" was a perfectly natural one for the Hebrews to apply to God. They were themselves a nation of shepherds. So, as early as the days of the patriarch Jacob, we find the name applied to God. But if it was natural for the people as a whole —because predominantly they were a pastoral people—it was doubly natural on David's lips, for he had been a shepherd himself. The old man's most vivid recollections are not those of recent happenings, but of those of his youthful days. He can remember the events of forty years ago better than he can those of a fortnight past. In this Psalm David is back again in those happy days when as a lad he used to keep the sheep of his father Jesse in the fields and on the hills of Bethlehem. He remembered what care he used to take that they should be properly fed and how on burning days of heat he used to lead them to quiet spots where they could refresh themselves with shade and water. And he remembered, too, how he had to guard them against the attacks of savage beasts. Two occasions came back vividly to his mind, the one when he had to fight with a lion and the other when he had to fight with a bear, each of which had taken a lamb out of the flock, and how he had killed both and rescued the living but terrified lambs out of their jaws. And, looking back over his own life beset by perils and dangers as it had been, David feels that God had protected him and cared for him just as he, in those far, off days, had protected and cared for his father's sheep. " The Lord is my shepherd."

Now, to appreciate the full force of the statement in this opening clause, you must always

remember that the " shepherd " David is thinking of is such a shepherd as he himself had
been. I have no word to speak by way of dis-
paragement to speak of our shepherds of today,
they are, speaking generally, kindly, helpful,
compassionate men. But in the nature of
things there could not be between our shepherds and their sheep the kind of tender, personal relation there was between the Eastern
shepherd and his sheep. You perhaps remember how F. W. Robertson, preaching on the
text, "I am the good shepherd," emphasizes
this point. He says: "You must try to feel
what the lowly Syrian shepherd must feel
towards the helpless things which are the com-
panions of his daily life, for whose safety he
stands in jeopardy every hour, and whose value
is measurable to him, not by price, but by his
own jeopardy, and then we have some notion
of the love the Psalmist meant to represent, the
Eternal Tenderness which bends over us and
knows the name of each, the trials of each, and
thinks for each with a separate solicitude, and

gave Himself for each with a sacrifice as special and a love as personal as if in the whole world's wilderness there were none other but that one." That is true, you must try to imagine all that. All that God is to us. "The Lord is my shepherd."

"*My* shepherd"—it is a personal and individual relationship. The emphasis of the Bible is ever on the individual. The modern tendency (perhaps, indeed, it always has been the tendency) is to lose sight of the unit in the crowd; to merge the individual in the mass. It is only a few highly placed or greatly gifted individuals who seem worth counting separately. But the Bible individualizes. It personalizes. God loves not masses, but men, individual men. God has an eye for the unit, for the humblest and most modest unit. "This poor man cried; the Lord heard him." His care is an individual care. His love is a personal love. "He calleth his own sheep by name." Do you remember how St. Paul, contemplating Christ's cross, takes that mighty sacrifice all to himself and cries, " The Son of God loved me and gave himself for me! " Calvary was all for him, he says. And he implies that if he had been the only lost sinner in the world Christ would have thought it worth His while to bear that cross in order to redeem him. But it is not alone a great Apostle like St. Paul who can say it. You and I can say it. The humblest of God's human creatures can say it. For our Lord has told us the same thing Himself. He said one day that if out of his flock of a hundred sheep but one had gone astray, that He would have gone after that *one* until He found it. One! Yes, if that one had been you or I, the Lord would have gone out into that wilderness in which He felt desolate and homeless and He would have climbed that hill on which He shed His blood in order to find us. The Lord's love is an individual love and His redemption is an individual redemption.

And what is true of the Son is equally true of the Father. It is all set forth in this little phrase: " The Lord is my shepherd." God's relation to you and me and all men is a personal and individual relation. And herein consists the real greatness of man—the real greatness of the most insignificant of men—he is great enough for God's individual love and care. It is of no use trying to prove to me the greatness of man by saying that one man wrote an *Iliad* and another a *Hamlet* and another a *Paradise Lost;* that one man painted a *Sistine Madonna* and another composed a *Hallelujah Chorus* and another built a St. Paul's Cathedral. These statements bring me no assurance of *my* greatness and worth. For the men who accomplished these things were geniuses, they did not belong to the common run of men. The average man knows well enough that Iliads and Hamlets and Hallelujah Choruses and St. Paul's Cathedrals are clean beyond him. What of this average man, this commonplace man, this man whose fame has not spread to the next street? And not only what of the average man, but what of the utterly insignificant man, the absolutely sunken and degraded man?

How great is he? Well, he is great enough for God's individual love and care. He is great enough for God to send His son to be born at Bethlehem and to die on Calvary for his sake. That is man's worth, your worth and my worth, and every man's worth. We are great enough for the measureless love and infinite sacrifice of God. It is all in this verse: "The Lord is my shepherd."

MAN'S FREEDOM FROM CARE

This is a tremendous statement about God. But David had found it to be literally true so far as he was concerned. Now look at the consequence for David of this mighty fact of the individual love and care of God. "The Lord is my shepherd, I shall not want. Therefore," is the Prayer Book rendering, "can I lack nothing." Moses, looking back over the forty years in the wilderness, declared to Israel, "These forty years the Lord thy God hath been with thee; thou hast lacked nothing." That was a wonderful testimony, but this is a more amazing assertion still. David's eye does more than sweep over the past, it takes in the future as well. "I shall not want." Because God cared for him with this individual love and care, therefore he could lack nothing—he could never be left bereft of anything he needed.

This little sentence, Bishop Perowne says, strikes the keynote of the Psalm. That keynote is one of serene and happy confidence. It is not the only place in the Bible where the note is struck. It is struck again and again in the Psalms. "In God will I put my trust," says another Psalm. "I will not be afraid, what can man do unto me?" "God is my salvation" says Isaiah. "I will trust and not be afraid." It is indeed one of the commonplaces of the old Book. But nowhere is it more beautifully stated than here. "The Lord is my shepherd . . . I shall not want." Take the two sentences together and they have all the force of an irrefragable argument. If the premiss of the first sentence is true, then the consequence of the second inevitably follows.

If the Lord is our shepherd, then we simply cannot want. For, you will notice, it is of "the Lord" this is said, the one and only Potentate, "King of kings and Lord of lords." It is the mighty Lord who is our shepherd. In Him, that is to say, love is combined with power. Love without power is not enough to give us quietness and rest. Love is mighty, but it is not omnipotent, and if it was only love that was caring we could not be sure that we should never want. Do you remember how helpless we were to assist Rumania in the hour of her bitter need? We badly wanted to help, but we couldn't. I suppose the mightiest human love is a mother's. But a mother's love cannot do what it wishes to do for, say, a sick child. But our shepherd is the mighty Lord. His power is as great as His love. There is no emergency in which He cannot help. There is no crisis in which His care is not sufficient.

I read again this last summer Alphonse Daudet's account of the passing of his friend

Edmond de Goncourt. "My wife," he says, "prayed and wept upon her knees at the foot of the bed. I, who knew no prayer, held his hand in mine, bending over him, my tears mingled with the death-dew upon his brow. I spoke to him quite low, quite clear. 'My friend, it is I; I am here quite close.' I do not know if he could hear me." There you have a picture of the impotence of human love in the supreme hour. But even then the mighty Lord can care. "When thou passest through the River I will be with thee." For all time, and for every experience that life can bring, we are safe in this guardianship. "The Lord is my shepherd. I shall not want." The man who knows that God is caring for him need have no cares about himself. "Be not anxious," Jesus said, "your Father knoweth." All things will work together for his good. And so we may have that assurance. We have but to commit ourselves into God's keeping and we, too, can say with David, "The Lord is my shepherd. I shall not want."

II

THE SHEPHERD'S LEADING

The Lord is my shepherd, no want shall I know;
  I feed in green pastures, safe-folded I rest:
He leadeth my soul where the still waters flow,
    Restores me when wandering, redeems when op-
      pressed.

Through the valley and shadow of death though I
      stray,
  Since Thou art my guardian no evil I fear;
Thy rod shall defend me, Thy staff be my stay;
  No harm can befall, with my Comforter near.

In the midst of affliction my table is spread;
  With blessings unmeasured my cup runneth o'er;
With perfume and oil Thou anointest my head:
  O what shall I ask of Thy providence more?

Let goodness and mercy, my bountiful God,
  Still follow my steps till I meet Thee above;
I seek, by the paths which my forefathers trod
  Through the land of their sojourn, Thy Kingdom
      of love.
                              —*James Montgomery.*

II

THE SHEPHERD'S LEADING

*" He maketh me to lie down in green pastures;
He leadeth me beside the still waters."*

IN the preceding chapter I had so much to
say by way of introduction that I had no
time to do anything like justice to the contents of that first verse with which I was supposed to be dealing. So before entering upon
the consideration of verse two, I want to turn
back for a moment and say a word or two
further about the great assertion with which
the Psalm opens. In speaking about God as
the shepherd, I laid the main stress upon the
tenderness and loving care of God which the
figure quite evidently suggests. But that is not
the only idea suggested by the figure. Dr.
Davison, in his admirable little commentary
upon the Psalms, insists upon it that more
prominent even than the ideas of care and ten-

derness are the ideas of strength and wisdom and authority. In the Old Testament the shepherd is essentially a ruler. The king, for instance, was the shepherd of his people. In that most precious of all allegories in which Jesus speaks of Himself as the good shepherd, while there is exquisite tenderness and love in it, there is also the unmistakable note of authority. Indeed it is on that note of authority He brings the allegory to a finish. So when we think of God as the shepherd, we must not emasculate the figure. There is force and vigour and power and authority in it as well as tender love.

We find extraordinary difficulty in combining together the ideas of power and gentleness, strength and tenderness, authority and grace, love and holiness. I suppose that is because in men they so seldom co-exist that we have come to look upon them as being mutually exclusive. It is a common saying amongst us that " a man suffers from the defects of his qualities." That is to say, if a man is conspicuously strong, he is very rarely gentle as well; if he is more than ordinarily forceful, he is not as a rule tender and considerate. On the other hand, if he is notable for his tenderness, he is not as a rule strong, and if he is more than usually gentle, he is as a rule lacking in force. The strong and forceful man is as a rule aggressive and rough. The tender and gentle person is as a rule yielding and soft. This is so much so that we have come to regard these qualities as being contradictories and therefore as being as mutually exclusive as light and darkness. But that is only because human nature as we see it is so partial and one-sided and incomplete. Our sin has warped and distorted this nature of ours. It was made in the image of God, but we have mutilated and disfigured it. In human nature as God meant it to be these various qualities that seem to us almost contradictory and exclusive, were meant to co-exist in perfect balance and equipoise. They do so co-exist in the one absolutely perfect life this world has seen. The characteristic of Jesus is His balance, the combination in Him of seemingly opposite

qualities. He is like that city which the seer
saw, of which he says that the length and
breadth and the height of it are equal. Jesus'
character was four-square like that. He was
strong, He was tender, He was self-assertive
and self-forgetful, He was authoritative and
He was humble, He was holy and He was
merciful. You can gather that contrasted
qualities existed side by side in the character of
Jesus from the guesses men made as to His
identity. For some thought He was Elijah
and others thought He was Jeremiah. Now,
two more contrasted characters than Elijah and
Jeremiah could not very well be conceived.
Elijah was all fire; Jeremiah was melting tenderness. Elijah was like a whirlwind; Jeremiah's head was a fountain of tears. And yet
to some people Jesus appeared like Elijah, and
to others He appeared like Jeremiah. The fact
is that the fire of the one prophet and the tenderness of the other met in Him. He was
Elijah when sweeping the mob of traffickers
out of the temple courts. He was Jeremiah

when weeping over Jerusalem's wayward and disobedient people. These seemingly contrasted qualities of strength and tenderness met in Him in perfect poise. And they meet similarly in the character of God. They are suggested by this title " shepherd," which is applied to Him here. There is more than the idea of tender care in it—there is strength and authority in it as well.

Indeed, as I said in the preceding chapter—though I had not sufficient space adequately to develop the thought—the truth that God is our shepherd would not comfort us very much if the only ideas it conveyed were those of love and tender care. If we are to enjoy protection and safety, our shepherd must not only be gentle, he must be brave; he must not only be tender, he must be strong. The literal shepherd had to be both. David himself had to be both. He could never have been a successful shepherd of his father Jesse's sheep if he had not been both. He had to be tender in his dealing with the sheep themselves; he had to be gentle

in his treatment of the ewes and the lambs.
But he had to be brave enough to stand up
against the wild beasts who threatened their
safety; he had to be strong enough to overcome any lion or bear that dared attack his
helpless charges. David was both—tender to
the sheep, terrible to the foes that threatened
their safety and their peace. *And our shepherd
is God.* In Him love and power unite; in
Him strength and tenderness are perfectly
blended. *Love by itself would not have been
sufficient.* Love is often baffled and beaten and
broken. Do you remember G. F. Watts'
picture "Love and Death" ? There Love is
depicted as a boy—a weak and tender boy—
Death is represented as a great and towering,
solemn figure, with strength in its every line.
And what can little Love do against that
mighty and ruthless giant? Love is powerless
to stay his course or to deny him entrance.
And that picture is just a parable. Love is
helpless against many of the foes that beset us
as we journey through life. Here is Love in

the person of a mother here at home, and away yonder in some distant land is a child fighting for life. What can Love do? Here is Love in the person of a father in a quiet little country home and away in the big town is a son beset by sore temptation, whose soul is amongst lions—what can Love do? Love often wants to help and cannot. Its power is not equal to its desire.

But in God there is power to do all that love desires. "Many are the afflictions of the righteous, but the Lord *delivereth him out of them all.*" There is in God strength to perform all that He wishes to do for us. "He delivereth him out of them all." He is able to save man from the foes that beset his way and lie in wait for his soul. He is able to save from the assaults of temptation. He is able to save from the power of sin. He is able to save in the hour of death. "He delivereth him out of them all." Our Shepherd is strong as well as gentle. The sheep are perfectly safe in His charge. "No one can pluck them out of my Father's hands."

Now the second verse—to which we are to turn our attention in our present study—has in it these ideas of wisdom and strength and authority, as well as of tender care. " He maketh me to lie down in green pastures, He leadeth me beside the still waters." In all this the shepherd just showed his shepherd's craft. There are some commentators who think that in verses two, three and four the Psalm describes the morning, afternoon and evening of the shepherd's day. But this reference to morning, afternoon and evening can only be secured by forced interpretation and by reading into the verses ideas which to the plain man do not appear to be there at all. I think we had better disregard all such explanations altogether as being artificial and purely imaginative. This verse two is not nearly so descriptive of the morning as it is of the fierce noonday and the sultry afternoon. What the shepherd who knows his business does when the sun is high in the heavens and the heat is fierce is this: he searches out some cool, green meadow by the water courses which cause the grass to grow, and there he causes his flock to lie down and rest. He is able to make them lie down in green pastures and to lead them by the still waters, because he knows all about that country-side. He has been over the ground, many a time, with the thought of the welfare of his flock ever in his mind. The wisdom of the shepherd is in all this, and his authority, too, for if he leads his flock into the green pastures it is because his sheep hear his voice and they follow him.

GOD'S NOURISHMENT

And all this is true of God. He is the shepherd who leads the flock into the green pastures and by the still waters. " Pastures . . . waters "—what do the two words suggest? Nourishment and support. That is what the sheep needs for its life—pasture and water. And that is the first thing a verse like this teaches me—that for the sustenance and support of his people, God richly provides. I turn to the New Testament allegory which is the counterpart of this Old Testament Psalm and I find Jesus saying this: " By me if any man enter in, he shall go in and go out and shall find pasture." It is exactly the same promise. God will amply provide for the support of those who obey Him and follow Him. I do not know which idea is most prominent in David's mind in this verse—whether physical or spiritual support. Probably both are there. There is a sense in which all people are the flock of God in that all men depend on Him for life and breath and all things. He makes grass to grow for the cattle and corn for the service of man. He brought Israel through the waste and howling wilderness, and they lacked nothing, for He rained down manna upon them from heaven and brought water for them from the living rock. And still He feeds and maintains His human children. We sit down every day to His table. He opens His hands and satisfies the desire of every living thing. He makes His sun to shine and His rain to fall on the just and the unjust. God never fails His children. Take the world as a whole and there is always enough and to spare for all its people.

But it was of the support of the soul that Jesus was mainly thinking in His allegory, and it is of that spiritual support I would speak for a minute or two. The Christian life—the life of discipleship to which the shepherd calls us— is a hard and strenuous life. It is a life that makes heavy demands upon us. If we are to live it at all, we need rich and constant support. You remember how, during rationing time, extra rations were allowed to men who had heavy and labourious work to do—the men in the shipyards and the engineering shops, for instance. The authorities realized that extra support was necessary for specially exhausting toil. Well, the Christian life makes extra and heavy demands upon a man as compared, say, with the ordinary, conventionally respectable life that passes muster with society. This latter life a man, perhaps, may live in his own

strength, but not the Christian life of purity
and sacrifice and service. We need extra
power if we are to live that life. And the
Shepherd sees to it that we get it. The fact is
that for the biggest and heaviest demand there
is always the sufficient grace. When the day
is extra trying, the Shepherd has always the
green pastures and still waters at hand for our
refreshment. What I mean, quite simply, is
this: that if we honestly commit ourselves to
the Christian life, God will see to it that the
support is forthcoming. We need not shrink
from it because of the difficulty—power more
than sufficient will be supplied.

"Pastures . . . still waters." And if you
ask me what are the pastures and still waters
by means of which God makes us equal to the
demands of the Christian life, well, perhaps I
may pass by other and lesser sources of nourishment and say simply Jesus Christ. "Pastures." "I," said He, "am the Bread of life."
"Still waters"? "Whosoever shall drink of
the water that I shall give him," He said,

"shall never thirst." Bread and water—the necessities of life and power are there in unlimited supply—we get them in Christ. That is to say, we get the strength to follow the Christ without by having a Christ within. The body feeds upon bread, but the soul is nourished and fed by Christ, and so nourished and fed it is equal to every emergency that life may bring. This is not empty rhetoric. It is just plain and sober fact. It is verified by human experience. Here, for instance, is one who cries, "I can do all things in Christ who strengtheneth me." He had had his full share of difficulty and trial and trouble, but he had overcome through Christ who loved him. There is, therefore, no need for us to cower and tremble before the difficulties of the Christian life, and there is no need to go on our way limping and enfeebled. In Christ God has prepared green pastures and still waters for the nourishment of the soul, and in Him we may have all sufficiency, always, for all things.

GOD'S KINDNESS

But I see more in this little verse than the promise of nourishment. I see in it a hint of the *kindness of God*. " He maketh me to lie down in green pastures; He leadeth me beside the still waters." " Green pastures . . . still waters." There is music in the very phrases. There is charm and beauty in the picture they conjure up before the mental vision. I wonder whether I am reading into it what I have no business to read into it when I suggest that the phrase declares that on the whole life is good? That is how David describes his life as he looks back on it. God had given him green pastures to lie down in and had led him by still waters. It wasn't that David had not had his troubles. He had had many, and they were deep and bitter. Yet he bears his witness that on the whole life had been an affair of " green pastures and still waters." I like the cheerfulness of this testimony, and I like it not simply because it is cheerful, but also because it is deeply and profoundly true. We have phrases in current use which describe life unfavourably —life is just a " vale of tears, it is a wilderness journey, it is a long exile." I think the modern tendency is to emphasize the sad and sorrowful and painful aspects of life, hence the pessimistic note that characterizes much of our present-day literature.

Now it would be foolish to ignore the fact that there is much that is sad and hard and painful in life. There come times to us when we are ready to assent to the dictum that life is a vale of tears and that the world is a desolate wilderness. But it is just as well that we should remember that on the whole the joys outbalance the sorrows, and the pleasures outbalance the pains. The reason why people are so apt to speak harshly and disparagingly of life is this: that pain makes a much deeper impression than joy. A week's illness will make us forget months and years of health. One worry will obliterate from our minds the memory of days which were full of pleasantness and peace. A grief will make us forget the years during which the family circle was unbroken. The fact is we take our happiness and health and family blessings as a matter of course, but when some blow comes upon us which robs us of one or the other of them, that one black cloud fills up all our horizon. But if we really took stock of things, we should find our blessings far outnumber our losses and griefs. We grumble about the weather. We cry out that it always rains. That is just sheer petulance. If we took the trouble to watch and count we should find the sun shines far oftener than the rain falls. The newspapers do us a distinct disservice in this regard. They emphasize the abnormal. They are full of dreadful stories of hate and bloodshed and adultery and theft. If you had only the newspapers to go by, you might think that all society was corrupt—a mass of wounds and bruises and festering sores. But as a matter of fact, the great mass of men are decent, kindly people who hate violence and wrong; the great majority of homes are marked by a quiet happiness and deep affection. Crime and lust are the abnormal, exceptional things. They command attention. They get talked about. But the honest, kindly people who do their duty to one another and to the state, never get talked about at all. But they are in the majority nevertheless.

When there is a crash on a railroad we talk of it for days, but we never mention the fact that every day the railways carry millions of people in safety. There is a sentence in one of the most familiar Psalms which says, "Forget not all His benefits." But that is exactly what we are prone to do. If we only did not forget, if we counted our blessings, we should find the benefits far outnumbered the deprivations, that the bright days outnumbered the dark days, and that pleasure far outbalanced pain. God cares not only for our subsistence, but for our happiness as well. This is a brave, cheerful retrospect of life, and it is as true as it is brave and cheerful. "Thou makest me to lie down in green pastures, thou leadest me beside the still waters."

WHAT ARE GREEN PASTURES?

But not only does a sentence like this suggest that life on the balance is a good and pleasant thing, but it suggests the further fact that what at the moment looked a bit of stony wilderness in the retrospect is seen to be a " green pasture." For this Psalm is a bit of retrospect. This is the old man David looking back and telling us what in the course of life he had found God to be. And that is his verdict as he looks back. Life under God's blessing and guidance had been an affair of " green pastures " and " still waters." But I do not think David would have said as much as that while events were actually in process—when he was being hunted by Saul like a partridge on the mountains, when he was treated as an outcast and an outlaw and was compelled to take service with the Philistines. I don't think he would have said he was being made to lie down in " green pastures." When pestilence smote his land, when hatred and murder penetrated his family circle, when Absalom rebelled against him and he had to flee for very life. I don't think he would have said he was being led beside the " still waters."

I think these things went sorely against the grain with him at the time. He would have escaped them if he possibly could. I wonder if it is at all fanciful to read a suggestion of compulsion and constraint into that phrase " thou makest me to lie down in green pastures " ? The shepherd, as one commentator says, stretches out the limbs of the sheep in order to make them repose. Perhaps the sheep would not have chosen that particular spot. The shepherd chooses it for it. " Thou *makest me* to lie down in green pastures." And God by the pressure and constraint of his Providence constrained David to pass through these troubled and troublous experiences of his. David would never have chosen them for himself. To him they appeared just sheer ills— bits of stony wilderness he would fain have avoided. But in what David thought a bit of stony wilderness God saw " green pastures."

In what David reckoned to be mere and sheer ills, God saw sources of blessing to the soul—so He made him to lie down in green pastures. For trouble and sorrow and loss, though they seem such harsh and forbidding things, provide often rich nourishment for the soul. "Tribulation worketh patience; and patience experience, and experience hope: and hope maketh not ashamed." "No chastening for the present seemeth to be joyous but grievous; nevertheless, afterward it yieldeth the peaceable fruit of righteousness unto them which are exercised thereby."

You remember how Greatheart in the Pilgrim describes the Valley of Humiliation as the best and most fruitful land in all those parts, and how that Mercy protested that she was as well in that Valley as she had been anywhere else in all their journey. That is only the old Dreamer's way of saying that bare and sterile places have often turned out to be "green pastures." And that is why God "makes us to lie down" in places from which we shrink. That is why He allows loss and trouble and disappointment to befall us. He knows what graces these things and their like beget in the soul, how they breed sympathy and tenderness and humility and dependence on God. They are indeed amongst the richest and most succulent pastures. And so God makes us to lie down in them in spite of ourselves. And later we come to recognize His wisdom. We realize the gain that has come to us. " It was good for me that I was afflicted." That was a man for whom the wilderness had been changed into the " green pastures." It is only in retrospect we recognize all this. While we are in the midst of life's hardnesses and difficulties and trials they may appear to us to be anything but " green pastures." But when we look back, in the mellow light of life's evening time, we shall realize we owe some of life's richest blessings to its troubled times, and shall be ready with David to confess " Thou makest me to lie down in green pastures, thou leadest me beside the still waters."

THE STILL WATERS

" Thou leadest me beside the still waters," or rather " by the waters of rest." It was rest, a resting place, Israel sought all through the forty years of wandering in the wilderness. They thought they would find it in Canaan. But they were disappointed. The fact is, the soul of man can never settle down and rest in any earthly home, it can only rest in God. And this Psalmist had found his centre. David had found his rest and peace in God. And that is still the shepherd's gift. He leadeth us beside the still waters. " Come unto me," He said, " all ye that labour and are heavy laden, and I will give you rest." And I wonder whether I am pressing the phrase too far when I say that here I get a hint of the end of the shepherd's guidance. He leads us to the waters of rest. There remaineth a rest for the people of God. You remember what the prophet says about the sea. " There is sorrow on the sea, it cannot be quiet." That is like life. It is always restless, stormy, troubled. There is a sea in the next world, but it is a sea of glass, on which no storm beats and no gale blows—a sea of glass mingled with fire—calm, untroubled, glorious. And to the shores of that sea, the shepherd will bring us at last, where the storm-tossed soul finds quiet and the restless heart finds peace. " He leadeth me beside the still waters."

III

RESTORATION AND GUIDANCE

The Lord my pasture shall prepare,
And feed me with a shepherd's care;
His presence shall my want supply,
And guard me with a watchful eye,
My noonday walks He shall attend,
And all my midnight hours attend.

When in the sultry glebe I faint,
Or on the thirsty mountain pant,
To fertile vales and dewy meads
My weary, wandering steps He leads
Where peaceful rivers soft and slow
Amid the verdant landscape flow.

Though in a bare and rugged way
Through devious, lonely wilds I stray,
Thy bounty shall my paths beguile;
The barren wilderness shall smile,
With sudden greens and herbage crowned,
And streams shall murmur all around.

Though in the path of death I tread,
With gloomy horrors overspread,
My steadfast heart shall fear no ill
For Thou, O Lord, art with me still;
Thy friendly crook shall give me aid,
And guide me through the dreadful shade.

—Joseph Addison.

III

RESTORATION AND GUIDANCE

*"He restoreth my soul: He leadeth me in the
paths of righteousness for His name's sake."*

I am not sure that the opening sentence of
this verse three does not properly belong to
verse two. At any rate, it attaches itself
closely to it and follows naturally and logically
upon it. Indeed the two clauses of verse two
and the opening clause of verse three form a
sequence, with this latter as a sort of climax.
" He maketh me to lie down in green pastures,
he leadeth me beside the still waters," and the
result and consequence is that " he restoreth
my soul." You must imagine a fiercely hot
Eastern day and the sheep becoming weary and
exhausted and spent. The wise shepherd,
under those circumstances, will lead them into
some cool and sheltered place where there is
food and drink to be had in order that they

may recruit their flagging energies and renew their strength. The purpose of the green pastures and the still waters is the restoration of the soul. Only " soul " is not exactly the word we should use in the case of the renewing of a sheep's energies. " Life " is the word we should have used of sheep. But in this Psalm, as Dr. Davison says, the natural and the spiritual, the symbol and the thing symbolized, are inextricably blended together and shade off into one another. And in this little phrase the thought of the shepherd and his sheep is almost submerged in the thought of God and man. That is why he says here " He restoreth my soul."

I cannot help thinking that back of this little phrase there lies a great experience. I cannot help thinking that David had a particular episode of his life in his mind when, but for God's love and care and concern, he might have lost his soul. And if you ask me what particular episode it was that David had in his mind, I reply it was that terrible and shameful episode of his sin with Bathsheba. David's soul was in peril many a time in the course of his life, but never in such dire and deadly peril as then. He sacrificed every consideration of honour and loyalty on the altar of his lust. He forgot his duty both to God and to his neighbour. He cast purity and honour to the wind, and recklessly plunged into sensuality and crime. If it had not been the Lord who was on his side, the waters had overwhelmed him, the stream had gone over his soul, then the proud waters had gone over his soul, and he would have been drowned in destruction and perdition. But the Lord was his shepherd and saw his danger and sent Nathan to him to rouse his sleeping conscience by the story of the rich man with his flocks and herds who robbed the poor man, his neighbour, of the one ewe lamb whom he had nourished and brought up, and which was to him as a daughter. "As the Lord liveth," said David, " the man that hath done this is worthy to die." And Nathan said to David, " Thou art the man." And beneath that terrible rebuke David saw his sin in all its shame and horror and humbled himself before God. He made his couch wet with tears and ate his bread with the bitter herbs of penitence and sorrow. And God's purpose in sending Nathan to stab his conscience wide-awake, and in allowing domestic grief to break his heart, was to restore his soul, to restore it to faith and honour and purity. Penitence, humiliation, grief,—these were the " green pastures " in which God made David lie down.

They did not look like " green pastures." They seemed harsh, ugly, forbidding places. David would never have chosen them for his resting-place. He would never have guessed that any refreshing could have been derived from them. God *made* him lie down in these things. He fed him with the bread of tears. He gave him the bread of adversity and the water of affliction. You notice these phrases, the " bread of tears "—tears can be bread to the soul, tears may be " green pastures." The " water of affliction "—affliction can be refreshing to the soul, affliction may be "waters of rest." This was the nutriment God gave David's sick and leprous soul. He gave him the bread of tears, He gave him the water of affliction. By penitence and humiliation and grief He purged David of his sin and brought him back to moral health. He made him to lie down in the "green pastures" of sorrow and repentance. He led him beside the still waters of affliction, and so He restored his soul, his sick and almost dying soul. This is a bit of personal experience and I detect in it the throb and thrill of a gratitude that he never forgot. "He restoreth my soul." David would have been a castaway, a moral derelict, a lost soul; he would have made his bed in hell but for the tender care and grace and wisdom and power of God. It was the Shepherd who saved this perishing sheep by bringing him to the green pastures and the still waters. He fed him with the bread of tears and gave him the water of affliction and so he restored his soul.

GOD THE RESTORER

"He restoreth my soul." Does language, *can* language convey to men a more heartening assurance than this? There the assertion stands, without qualification or exception of any kind, majestic in its simplicity. "He restoreth the soul." Not "some souls," but "the soul"; the soul wherever it is found, and that means your soul and my soul and every soul. "He restoreth *the soul*." He restores it! Doctors will sometimes tell their patients that they can *relieve* their sickness but cannot entirely cure it. There is no such reservation about this promise. No matter what the condition of the soul may be, God can restore it. He can not only minimize the mischief, He can *restore* the soul to perfect soundness and health. You remember Jeremiah's great proclamation to Israel—to an Israel tempted to think that its hurt was beyond healing and its pain incurable? This is what he had to say in God's name to that sinful people: "I will restore health unto thee and I will heal thee of thy wounds," saith the Lord. Jeremiah was only applying to a special and particular case the assertion of my text, " He restoreth my soul."

My *soul!* And my soul is the real *me*. It is the eternal part of me. Man *has* a body, but he *is* a soul. That is what the old Book says about him. " God breathed into his nostrils the breath of life; and man became a living soul." It is that soul, that heavenly spark, that Divine breath in him that makes him man. And it profits a man nothing if he gain the world and lose his soul. Now the very phrase, " He *restoreth* the soul," suggests that the soul may fall sick, that it may be smitten with disease, that it may be in danger of death. And the suggestion of the text is borne out by the actual experience of life. The world is full of sick souls, diseased souls, leprous souls, perishing souls. John, in his letter to Gaius, expresses the prayer that he may prosper and be in health even as his soul prospereth. If the measure of our soul health were also the measure of our physical health we should be a world of invalids. For most of us are sick souls, feeble, weak and fainting. And some are sick souls in the sense of being diseased, mortally stricken. Indeed, our world would be a pretty hopeless world but for the assurance of such a phrase as this—" He restoreth the soul." And this assurance is not an empty phrase. It is an assurance ratified by incontestable facts. God has been restoring souls all down the ages. God came into this world in the person of Jesus. And that was the work to which Jesus gave Himself, the work of restoring souls. " The spirit of the Lord is upon me," He said at Nazareth, " because He hath anointed me to preach good tidings to the poor; He hath sent me to proclaim release to the captives, and recovery of sight to the blind, to set at liberty them that are bruised." You notice the words " release," " recovery," to " set at liberty "—they all suggest aspects of " restoring " work. " The Son of Man," He said on another occasion, " is come to seek and to save that which was lost." To " seek and to save "—Jesus came to " restore," and He *did* restore. He restored many a person to physical health. He cleansed the leper. He gave sight to the blind, and hearing to the deaf, and power to the paralyzed, and life to the dead.

But His mightiest restoring ministry was His restoration of souls. Here, for instance, was a woman in one of the northern towns in whose soul all nobler and purer instincts had been drowned and submerged in sensual pleasures, a woman whose soul was all leprous with lust, a woman who was a sinner in the city, and Jesus somehow brought His love and grace to bear upon that sin-stained creature until all the love of sinful pleasure was purged out of her heart and her one passionate longing was to become clean and pure again. " He restored her soul." And here in Jericho was a man who was a chief tax-gatherer, and who had allowed greed so to engross his heart that he cheated and swindled and thieved and ground the faces of the poor without compunction or mercy. But Jesus came into the man's house and brought His love and grace to bear upon him and at the touch of Jesus the greed and the hardness of Zacchæus' heart disappeared, and pity and mercy and kindness and truth began to stir there once again. He "restored his soul." And here in Jerusalem was another man, a prominent and famous man, a religious leader, but who had allowed pride and prejudice and religious bigotry to make his heart as hard as a nether millstone, so that in persecuting Christ's people he thought he was doing God service, but as he travelled to Damascus Christ met with him and the result of that meeting was that Saul got a new heart and the persecutor became a Gospel preacher. Christ "restored his soul."

David is not the only one who gives this testimony. There is a multitude which no man can number out of every nation and kindred and tongue, who have washed their robes and made them white in the blood of the Lamb, every one of whom bears the same testimony, "He restoreth my soul." There is no disease of the soul that He has not been able to cure. No sickness of the soul which He has not been able to heal. Do you remember that passage in one of his letters to the Corinthians in which Paul gives a list of lost souls, people who cannot inherit the Kingdom of God? It is a terrible list. I wonder if I dare read it? " Neither fornicators, nor adulterers, nor idolaters, nor effeminate, nor abusers of themselves with men, nor thieves, nor covetous, nor drunkards, nor revilers, nor extortioners, shall inherit the Kingdom of God." " And such," he adds with terrible bluntness, " were some of you." Some of these very people to whom he was writing had been amongst the diseased, defiled and mortally stricken souls of that sort. But something wonderful, something almost incredible, had happened to them. " But ye were washed, but ye were sanctified, but ye were justified in the name of the Lord Jesus Christ and in the Spirit of our God." These sunken, degraded, perishing people had been restored to moral health by the power of Christ. He had " restored" their souls. To the cleansing and curative power of a physician who can accomplish such miracles as these, no task of healing is impossible. His blood can make the foulest clean. He can wash white the most defiled and polluted soul. And in the soul that has wallowed in the very mire of sin, He can cause purity and truth and love to grow and flourish. He can restore the soul to what it was meant to be. He can give it joy and peace and abounding health.

"He restoreth *my* soul," says the Psalmist. The restoring power of God was more to him than a general truth, it was an individual experience. "My soul"! In a sense all Christ's cleansing and saving power avails us nothing until we put ourselves into His hands. It will profit us nothing to read about His miracles of healing grace unless we let Him exercise that grace upon us. We know nothing of the joy of salvation until we can say, not "He restoreth *the* soul," but "He restoreth *my* soul." But if we come to Him as we are, poor, wretched, and blind, we shall get from Him " sight, riches, healing of the mind," and then we shall be able to say exultingly, triumphantly with the Psalmist in the text, " He restoreth *my* soul."

THE CONVENIENT FOOD

God is the great Restorer, and there is no soul in the world beyond His restoring power. But perhaps it was not that wide interpretation of God's power that was mainly in the Psalmist's mind. The figure before him is that of the shepherd and his flock. It is the fainting and wearied sheep of his own flock the shepherd " restores." And possibly the thought that was primary in the Psalmist's mind was that of God's ability to restore those of His own people who had fainted and grown weary. That was the case with David himself. His shameful fall was the fall of one who knew God and professed to serve Him. But God in His infinite mercy did not cast him away for his sin—He " restored " him. In later days

Peter denied his Lord with oaths and curses in the judgment hall. Jesus did not wash His hands of His weak and treacherous disciple. With exquisite patience and love, He strengthened his faith and made him equal to the great tasks of Apostleship—He "restored" him. And God's people still falter and fail. They grow weary, fainting in their souls. They lose their first love. Their early enthusiasm dies down. "Where is the blessedness I knew when first I saw the Lord?" It is the cry of one whose soul had somehow lost tone and vigour and health. But God "restores" the soul. He can strengthen the faint and weary. He can revive drooping energies. He can bring back the glow and ardour of the first devotion. There are many things that affect the health of the soul. But the suggestion of my text is that the soul is "restored" by being provided with the proper food. "He maketh me to lie down in green pastures, he leadeth me beside the still waters, he restoreth my soul." It is the green pastures and the still waters that account for the restoration. Our souls are like our bodies in this respect, that their health depends upon convenient food.

I have been reading lately Sir Ernest Shackleton's *South,* and one of the most poignant narratives in the book is the story of the party who went depot-laying from the Aurora. They did fairly well on the outward journey. But on the homeward march they almost suffered the fate that befell Captain Scott. Of the six men who made the party three were ill and had to be carried on sledges. The other three would not have minded that had they themselves been strong. Indeed they did not mind it, weak though they were. But it was terrible work. For sometimes they were so reduced for food that all they could have for breakfast was a cup of tea and half a biscuit, and for lunch a half-cup of weak tea and quarter of a biscuit, while the poor dogs were left together for days without any food at all. And then, weak as they were, they suffered from frost-bite, and finally scurvy attacked them. It became a grim fight for life, for their own lives and for the lives of their helpless comrades on the sledges. And there is one cry that rings through the various notes in the leader's diary, it is the cry for food, and a food of the right kind. Here is a sample entry: "Hayward is getting worse, and one does not know who is the next. No mistake, it is scurvy, and the only possible cure is fresh food!" Here is another: "Hayward and Skipper going ahead on sticks at a very slow pace. I wonder what will be the outcome of it all. If one could only get some fresh food!" Nothing else the leader knew would set right the blackened, swollen, scurvy-stricken bodies of his comrades.

And the soul needs convenient food if it is to be kept in health. The reason why so many of our souls are feeble and sickly is that we are trying to feed them with unsuitable food. We try to satisfy them with mere things. You remember what the rich man said to his soul: "Soul," he said, "thou hast much goods laid up for many years; eat, drink, be merry." He imagined he could feed his soul with " goods." And many—judging by their practice—believe the same thing. They make " goods " their aim. They seem to think they can be happy and content if they have " goods " in plenty. Even people who are nominally Christian seem more concerned about " goods " than they are about anything else. But you cannot feed the soul with " goods." You cannot satisfy the soul with things. That is a striking and suggestive word in which our Lord, describing those represented by the seed which fell into the thorny ground, said that they were men and women whose spiritual life, whose souls, were choked with cares and riches and pleasures of this life. The soul is not nourished by these things, it is simply " choked " by them, starved by them, debilitated by them. It is exactly in the same condition as the bodies of those Antarctic explorers were, who were frost bitten, blackened with scurvy and at the extremity of weakness for lack of fresh food. And all this is matter of experience. We can see the growing enfeeblement and impoverishment of the souls of those whose devotion is given to the riches and pleasures of this life. And the reason for this is quite obvious. God has put eternity in the heart of man. The soul of man is athirst for God, for the living God. You cannot nourish the eternal soul on "goods." Man cannot live by bread alone. The soul needs God. Jesus Christ is the soul's food. It is by communion with Him, by sharing His life, that it is truly and properly fed. It is in Christ we find the "green pastures," and the "still waters" which refresh and revive and enlarge the soul. "I am the Bread of life." "He that drinketh of the water which I shall give him shall never thirst." And that is how God "restores the soul," brings it back to vigour and health again, by leading it to the green pastures and still waters to be found in Christ.

PATHS OF RIGHTEOUSNESS

"He restoreth my soul. . . . He guideth me

in the paths of righteousness for his name's sake." After the *restoring* comes the *guiding*. After the rest comes further effort. The shepherd took the sheep down into the green pastures and the still waters to refresh them in the time of fierce and sultry heat, but the green pastures and the still waters were not to be their permanent abode. He led them there to restore their energies and to renew their strength, in order that they might be fit to follow him when he guided them along straight paths either to their fold or to some further pasturage. And God brings to us in Christ the bread of life and the water of life in order to " restore our souls," so that then He may be able to guide us into " paths of righteousness," into ways of service and duty. We come to Christ to have our souls nourished and fed, and then He sends us out onto the road again—the hot and dusty road—going His errands and accomplishing His work. The Good Shepherd had to " restore " us before He could guide us into paths of righteousness. Until we were so "restored" we should have no strength to follow.

Let me go back to my Antarctic illustration again. At a certain point the leader resolved he would leave the sick behind with one man to care for them, while he and two others made a dash for a depot thirty miles away, where food was stored. Until they were properly fed it was hopeless to expect the sick men to make the rest of the journey. So back and fore they went, bringing ample rations with them and having first restored the strength of their sick comrades they were able to bring them in safety to the depot which was to be their winter's home. First the restoration, then the straight path home. And it is very much the same with Christ and the soul. We could not follow along the paths of righteousness—the narrow way of life and duty—before we were "restored," strengthened with might in our souls. But once we are "restored," He guides us into paths of righteousness. Refreshment is meant to issue in effort. "He called twelve," it is written in the Gospel, " that they might be with Him." During these months and years of happy companionship the disciples were in green pastures and by still waters, and their souls were verily being " restored." But " restoration " was meant to lead to service. " He called twelve that they might be with Him and *that He might send them forth.*" When renewed and restored, He meant to lead these men out along paths of duty and service and sacrifice and martyrdom. When on the holy mount Peter and James and John saw their Lord transfigured, the three disciples were verily in the green pastures and by the still waters. They were privileged and favoured men, and by the experience their souls were confirmed and strengthened and inspired. " Master," cried Peter, " it is good for us to be here; let us make three tabernacles, one for Thee and one for Moses and one for Elijah." But the " restoration " was meant to lead to effort, and so in the morning Jesus led them down again to the plain at the foot, where there was urgent work to be done and devil-ridden sufferers to be healed. " He restoreth my soul, He guideth me in the paths of righteousness."

Or to look at it from a slightly varying point of view, the recovery of the soul is meant to issue in a life of obedience and discipleship. Conversion is not the end, it is the beginning. Zacchæus' soul was restored when Jesus entered his home. But the little man after that experience began to realize that Christ was leading him along a certain path—it was a steep and difficult path—the path of righteousness, but he followed. " Lord," he said, " the half of my goods I give to the poor, and if I have taken anything from any one by false accusation, I restore four fold." None but the " restored soul " can tread that high and arduous way, but when the Shepherd has " restored " our souls it is along that high and arduous way He guides us. And the proof that our souls are " restored "- is that we bravely tread that steep and perilous " path of righteousness." In other words, a holy life is the evidence of a changed heart. " He *guideth* me in the paths of righteousness." The Shepherd does not *drive;* He *guides.* " When He hath put forth all his own he goeth before them and the sheep follow Him." If He guides us along steep and rugged ways, at any rate we have the comfort of knowing He is in front. He never says to His people " Go." It is always " Come." It is easy to follow when we hear His voice. And if we follow along that path of righteousness which He so bravely trod and along which He leads, it will bring us where it brought Him, even though it is through Gethsemanes and Calvarys, to the city which hath the foundations, to the throne and the crown and the very Presence of God.

IV
THE VALLEY

My Shepherd's mighty aid,
   His dear, redeeming love,
His all-protecting power displayed,
   I joy to prove:
Led onward by my Guide
   I view the verdant scene,
Where limpid waters gently glide
   Through pastures green.

In error's maze my soul
   Shall wander now no more;
His Spirit shall, with sweet control,
   The lost restore;
My willing steps shall lead
   In paths of righteousness;
His power defend; His bounty feed
   His mercy bless.

Affliction's deepest gloom
   Shall but His love display;
He will the vale of death illume
   With living ray:
My failing flesh His rod
   Shall thankfully adore;
My heart shall vindicate my God
   For evermore.

His goodness ever nigh,
   His mercy ever free,
Shall, while I live, shall when I die,
   Still follow me;
For ever shall my soul
   His boundless blessings prove;
And while eternal ages roll
   Adore and love.

                —*Thomas Roberts.*

IV

THE VALLEY

"Yea, though I walk through the valley of the shadow of death, I will fear no evil; for thou art with me; Thy rod and Thy staff they comfort me."

I must crave indulgence while I do again, in this chapter, what I have already done once before—go back to the verse which I was supposed to have dealt with in the previous chapter, before I pass on to the verse which is to be the special subject of our present study. I found so much to say about that first clause in verse three, "He restoreth my soul," that I left myself no time to do anything like justice to the second clause, "He guideth me in the paths of righteousness," while about the third clause, "for His name's sake," I was able to say nothing at all. So I want to be allowed to return to verse three for a moment or two and say just a few things which properly belong to the last chapter.

" He guideth me in the paths of righteousness," the Psalmist says, and some commentators are inclined to say that " paths of righteousness " mean simply " straight paths." Now it is quite true that this meaning is included in the phrase. If we allow the Good Shepherd to guide us, He will lead us along " straight paths," paths which will bring us safely to the home and haven of our souls. It is not always easy to pick out the right road as we journey through life. We come now and again to crossroads, and what is more dangerous still, to roads that seem to run side by side, and it is quite easy, as Christian and his companion discovered, to get astray from the right road. Life with its alternatives and its choices and its competing claims is often extraordinary puzzling. One of the Psalmists gives expression to the bewilderment of his soul in that pathetic little cry, " Make Thy way plain before my face." He was quite sure God had a way for him, and he was quite sure that way was the right way, but his difficulty was to make out which of several ways was really God's way. " Make Thy way plain," he prays, " before my face." And one of the great services which Messiah was to render to mankind, one of the great blessings which was to accompany His coming, was this. " He shall make the crooked places straight." The path a man ought to take was to be made unmistakable for him. And that has been done for us by Jesus Christ.

We are no longer in any difficulty about the road. He has made it plain before our face. For He has left marks upon it. When those Antarctic adventurers, to whom I have previously referred, were pushing their way into the bitter, frozen South at intervals they built cairns of ice and snow, and sometimes stuck a bit of black cloth upon them, that they might be able to trace their way back again. And the path of life has been marked for you and me so that we may not lose our way. Only the signs on it are not black, but red, like those great red splashes that mark the road over Mount

Tiflis down to Engleberg. For there are footprints on it, "bearing trace of having bled."
They are the footprints of Him who was crim-
son in His apparel and who came with dyed
garments from Bozrah. They are the footprints of the Good Shepherd Himself. There
is no mistaking the road. If we walk in the
track of these footprints they will bring us by
the right way to the city which hath the foundations whose builder and maker is God.

But while the idea of "straight paths" is
certainly in the phrase, I do not think it can be
limited to that geographical meaning. It has a
moral significance as well. For men, as Dr.
Maclaren says, straight paths must needs be
"paths of righteousness." Indeed that very
word "straight," in our common use of it,
when we apply it to men, carries with it a
moral signification. When we speak of a man
as "straight," we mean that he walks in "paths
of righteousness." And that is what the Shepherd does with the "restored soul." He leads
him into ways of holy living. When Christ

has won a man's heart, He bids him follow Him. "Come ye after me," He says, and it is along these high paths of obedient, pure, sacrificial living that He leads him. I do not want to read too much into the word "righteousness." I do not, for instance, want to read Paul's meaning into it. Righteousness, in the characteristically Pauline use of the word, means setting a guilty sinner right with God, making a sinful man righteous in the eyes of God. It is only Christ who can guide into that path of righteousness. It is only through Him we get pardon and reconciliation. But these ideas are not in the Psalmist's mind. He is thinking of "righteousness" in the sense of right doing and holy living. When Christ restores the soul, He leads it into new and loftier ways of life. To the man who has been born again by the proclamation of the Christian Gospel, Christ presents the demand of the Christian ethic. You have noticed how largely the Epistles are taken up with instructions as to the moral demands of the Christian life, plain and homely directions as to conduct? That is just a commentary on the statement of this verse. When Jesus " restores a soul," He does not allow that soul to go on in the old selfish, sensual ways. He guides it into paths of righteousness. After He had restored the soul of Onesimus, for instance, He gave his life a new set and direction. He made him honest, faithful, willing, reliable. He guided him into paths of righteousness. And so He does for us all. If any man is in Christ he is a new creature. Conversion issues in a new life. When Christ restores a man's soul He then guides him into paths of righteousness.

FOR HIS NAME'S SAKE

What an immensity of pains Christ takes with and for His sheep! What an infinitude of tender care all this represents! The Shepherd —and it makes very little difference whether you think of the Shepherd as God or as Christ —according to the Psalmist's jubilant confession, makes him to lie down in green pastures, leads him beside the still waters, restores his soul, and leads him into paths of righteousness. And why does God do all this? Why does He take all this trouble and care? Why this unceasing exercise of tenderness and love? He does it all, the Psalmist says, "for His name's sake," for the sake of His own character. "He does it," says Bishop Perowne, "not for our deserving, but out of His own goodness, for the manifestation of His own glory and the furtherance of His Kingdom upon earth." "God does many things for His name's sake," says Dr. Davison, "that He may be true to His own character, for He cannot deny Himself." It is not because the sheep are precious and valuable (though no doubt they are all that) that the Shepherd takes all this care of them, but because His own Shepherd instincts constrain Him to do it. It is not because we are precious in His sight (though He condescends to count us such) that God takes the trouble to feed and sustain and restore and guide us, but just because He is what He is—a God of infinite compassion and tender love. He does it " for His name's sake."

It was for " His name's sake " that He sent His only Son into the world to live and die for our salvation. It was not for our sake He did it. There was nothing in us to arouse a love like that. We had rebelled against Him; we were sin-stained and unclean. We were alienated from God by our wicked works. If it had depended on our desert, there never would have been an Incarnation or an Atonement. The impulse to the redeeming mission of the Son came from the Father's love. " God so loved the world that He gave His only begotten Son." It was to satisfy the yearning of God's heart that Jesus came. The Gospel originates not in the fact that men wanted God, but that God wanted men. It was " for His own name's sake " that God sent His Son.

It is " for His name's sake " that God forgives us and receives us into His household. It is not *for our sakes*. There is nothing in us to merit mercy and favour like this. For we are wayward, perverse and disobedient children. We do not deserve mercy. We are not worthy to be called His children. It is " for His own name's sake " that He forgives us and receives us and gives us the kiss of welcome—just because He is the Lord, full of compassion and gracious, slow to anger and plenteous in mercy and truth.

And if at last we attain to the mansions of the blest, it will not be for our own sakes, because we are so good and holy that we deserve admission; it will be again " for His name's sake." It will be all of grace, not of merit, it will be because His wonderful love opens the door to us, though unworthy.

And I am glad that it is for " His name's sake " God does all these things. I am glad that it is " for His name's sake " He supports and sustains and restores and guides us. God's character is an infinitely surer thing to rely upon than our own. It is to that character of God the saints of all ages have appealed; it is in it they have trusted and on it they have quietly rested. For instance, if they have cried for the pardon of their sins, it has been " for His name's sake." "For Thy name's sake pardon mine iniquity, for it is great." If they have wanted tender and gentle dealing it is for God's name's sake they have dared to ask for it, not because they deserved it. " Deal Thou with me, for Thy name's sake." Men have known—and the best men have been the most vividly aware of this—that they had no claim by their own merit or desert on the favour and love of God. In strict justice not one of us should see salvation. Their hope has been not in themselves, but in God; not in what they are, but in what He is; not in works, but in faith; not in merit, but in grace.

Here is the true anchor of the soul. Here is the sure ground of confidence, the spring of triumphant assurance. God's mercy and love and care are forthcoming *for His name's sake.* God has to live up to His own character. I confess to you, my brethren, if mercy and love and care were contingent on a certain character of my own, I should despair. If, for instance, my acceptance with God depended on a certain holiness of my own, I should abandon hope. It is only a morally obtuse braggart like Rousseau who, with the record of his life in his hands, would talk about claiming acquittal at the bar of God as a matter of right. Our own hearts condemn us. We know quite well that our lives are full of evil. No, there is no acceptance for me because of what I am, but I humbly believe that I shall be accepted because of what *God* is, because His is a love that forgives to the very uttermost. If, again, my walking in straight paths depended on myself, on my resolution and strength of will, I should despair. For I know myself fickle, inconstant, changeable. One day I walk firmly in the narrow way; another I love to choose my own path. One day my devotion is warm, another it is cold and dead. If it depended on myself I should be more than doubtful of ever reaching the City which hath foundations. But when I remember God, I have my hopes that I shall be privileged to see that city whose streets are gold, whose walls are jasper and whose sea is glass. For God is constant and unchanging, and He has charged Himself with my care. There is no fickleness about God. He is no creature of moods. His love never grows cold. His care never falters. We may become faithless, but He abideth faithful. We may forget Him, but He never forgets us. Our hold of Him may relax, but never His hold of us. He will never leave us nor forsake us until He has accomplished that which concerneth us. And that, I repeat, is our confidence that there will always be mercy and acceptance and guidance and keeping grace for us. God, as the Apostle says, cannot deny Himself. He must act in accord with His character, and His character is one of redeeming and sacrificial love. Because God is what He is, if we will commit ourselves to Him, He will forgive and guide and keep and save. "He maketh me to lie down in green pastures, He leadeth me beside the still waters; He restoreth my soul; He guideth me in the paths of righteousness, *for His name's sake.*"

THE VALLEY OF GLOOM

Now the next verse, as it seems to me, connects itself quite closely with the concluding clause of verse three. It could never have been penned but for the thoughts of God's love and unfailing care suggested by that little phrase, "for His name's sake." This verse four brings us to the climax of the Psalmist's confidence. It is a great outburst of triumph. It reminds me of that thrilling shout of victory which St. Paul raises in the great resurrection chapter in his first letter to the Corinthians when, facing the last enemy, he cries, "O death, where is thy sting? O grave, where is thy victory? Thanks be to God, which giveth us the victory through our Lord Jesus Christ." There is not, perhaps, the same exuberance in what the Psalmist says here—that could scarcely be expected, seeing that he did not live in the light of the resurrection of Christ. The tone of this verse is not, perhaps, one of exuberant triumph; it is rather one of serene and quiet confidence. And it is the thought of God's nature and character that has inspired it. " Yea, though I walk through the valley of the shadow of death, I will fear no evil; for Thou art with me; Thy rod and Thy staff they comfort me." It is distasteful to me to have to suggest that a translation which has by long use become familiar and dear to us, does not quite accurately reproduce the Psalmist's thought. But you will notice that in the Revised Version margin, the alternative rendering is suggested, " the valley of deep darkness." There is no doubt at all that that is the more accurate translation. The rendering " valley of the shadow of death," unduly narrows and limits the phrase. Death is not the only " valley of gloom " into which we are led as we pass through life. It may be the gloomiest—though I have my doubts on that point. But there are certainly other valleys of gloom, as, for instance, sickness and loss of friends and business anxiety. And what the Psalmist is saying here is not simply that he will not fear when death comes, but that he will not fear when he is called upon to enter any "valley of deep gloom" that may have to be traversed in the course of life's journey.

The picture is one of the shepherd leading his sheep through some dark and sunless ravine in the hills, and the sheep following quite unafraid, because of their confidence in the shepherd, who with his rod—his club or mace for defence against the attacks of wild beasts—hanging at his side and his staff, for the guidance and help of his sheep, actually in his hand made himself responsible for their safety. In exactly the same way the Psalmist declares that he will be afraid of no ravine of gloom through which he may be led, because he is absolutely sure of the guidance and protection of God. "Thou art with me, Thy rod and Thy staff they comfort me."

What a contrast in scenery there is between verse two and verse four. In verse two the

Psalmist talked of "green pastures" and "waters of rest." Here he talks of the "ravine of deep gloom." And how true this is to life. For life does bring us varied experiences of this sort. It does change—sometimes in an instant—from sunshine to storm, from blue skies to black, from glory to gloom, and from green pastures and still waters we find ourselves suddenly walking in some valley of deep darkness. David again here is setting down his own experience. He had passed through many a ravine of deep gloom—those days of exile and outlawry, for instance, when he was hunted by Saul; those days of his family troubles consequent upon his own sin and the sin of his sons; those terrible days of Absalom's rebellion, when well nigh his whole kingdom fell away from him; and that worst of all days when the news was brought to him that his son Absalom was dead. And yet, looking back, he is conscious that in those "ravines of gloom" God was with him, caring for him and protecting—so whatever "valley of deep darkness" yet lay in front—and the valley of the shadow of death could not be very far off—he could face it without fear, confident that God would be with Him still, to keep and save. I say the contrasted scenes of these two verses are true to life. I do not withdraw what I said in a previous chapter about the preponderance in life being on the side of pleasure, not of pain. There is more of sunshine than of storm. If we struck a balance we should find that our days of quiet happiness outnumber our days of grief and sorrow. Life for the major part is an affair of green pastures and waters of rest. But it would be the foolishest and falsest of all affectations to pretend that life was nothing but sunshine and song—that it was nothing but smiles and gaiety. Trouble and sorrow and care and pain are very real things. No amount of pretending will get rid of them. And trouble and sorrow and care and pain come to us all at one time or another. Sooner or later we all find ourselves in the valley of deep gloom. Some of us—most of us, I suppose—at one

time or another have been in it. Some of you
have had your *times of sickness*. It was a
"valley of deep gloom." It was not simply
the pain you yourself had to endure, but your
concern for your loved ones; your anxiety for
the wife and children dependent on you. And
some of you have had your times of *business
anxiety*. It was a "ravine of deep gloom."
Many are in that "ravine" just now. A year
ago business seemed flourishing and business
men were in the green pastures. Today the
world of business is rocking beneath their feet,
and they do not know what is going to happen.
They are in the valley of deep gloom. And
some of you have had heavy and heart-breaking
sorrows. Your nearest and best have been
taken from you. You lost the light of your
life, the desire of your eyes at a stroke. I met
a close friend of mine the other day and he
said to me, "I want five minutes with you."
I said, "All right. Come upstairs." I sat
down with him in a corner of the room. And
there he broke down and in a series of little

heart-broken gasps he told me that the doctors had passed sentence on his wife, and would I come to see her? And somehow the day seemed to grow dark as I listened to him. I was with my friend in the "ravine of deep gloom."

There is no need to amplify, is there? These "valleys of deep darkness" have to be traversed by us all in the course of life's pilgrimage. But the assurance of my text is this: that we need not fear them—at least we need not fear that any evil will befall us. I do not suggest that sickness and care and sorrow are not fearful things—they are. The Psalmist does not say that, facing them, he knew no fear at all. What he does say is that the remembrance of God lifted him above his fear and made him quite sure that these fearful things could work him no harm. And that same assurance may be ours if we commit ourselves to the keeping care of God. Sickness and care and loss may, as a matter of fact, inflict terrible harm upon men. They have done harm to thousands, they have made them hard and sour and bitter and cynical. But if we are in God's keeping, we need fear no evil. These dread and terrible things will not be able to hurt us; they will be constrained to minister to our enrichment. You remember what the old Book says about wisdom? "Her ways are ways of pleasantness and all her paths are peace." And that is exactly what we shall say about God's ways, when we look back, even though they led us through "ravines of gloom." His ways were ways of pleasantness and all His paths were peace.

THE KEEPING PRESENCE

The secert of the Psalmist's confidence was the assurance of God's Presence. "Even though I walk through the valley of the shadow of death, I will fear no evil, for Thou art with me." It was not due to any trust in himself, but to his faith in God's keeping care. The antidote to fear, as one of the commentators puts it, is a Presence. Some trust to their own resolution and strength to see them safely through these "ravines of gloom." You remember how Henley sings proudly, almost defiantly, " I am the master of my fate, I am the captain of my soul." But our own strength is a poor thing to rely on. I do not deny that there is something fine and admirable about the way in which some men will string themselves up to bear trial and trouble—all the stings and arrows of outrageous fortune—without whimpering or whining. But not every one is a stoic. And I am not sure that the stoic temper, by begetting a certain hardness and callousness, does not itself do harm. No, the antidote to fear is a Presence. That is why we need fear no evil—from care or sickness or loss —because God will be with us; because His love will be about us; because His strength will be imparted to us, and strengthened by His power and comforted by His love we shall find that these harsh and unpleasant things have contributed to our moral and spiritual wealth.

And when it comes to the last " ravine " of all we may preserve our happy confidence. I say again that I am not sure that it is the darkest of the ravines of gloom we have to traverse. It is significant that John Bunyan puts the Valley of the Shadow of Death quite early in Christian's pilgrimage, as if to suggest that the worst peril does not come at the end. Nor does it, as I think. Death is not the dreadful thing we think it. "There is no valley here," said D. L. Moody. "At evening time, it shall be light." But most men dread it. And so this word is welcome to us with its calm assurance of faith. We need not fear that last ravine of gloom. It can work us no ill. For God will be with us. In death, as in life, we shall be in His safe protection and care. It is in God our trust is in death, as in life. Not in ourselves, but in Him. "Neither death nor life shall be able to separate us from the love of God which is in Christ Jesus our Lord." God is stronger than death. No! we need not fear. That last ravine of gloom is no *cul de sac*. Through it God leads to the land where there is no night, but sacred, high, eternal noon.

V

THE FULL TABLE

My Shepherd shall supply my need,
　　Jehovah is His Name;
In pastures fresh He makes me feed,
　　Beside the living stream.
He brings my wandering spirit back,
　　When I forsake His ways;
And leads me, for His mercy's sake,
　　In paths of truth and grace.

When I walk through the shades of death—
　　His presence is my stay;
A word of His supporting breath,
　　Drives all my fears away.
His hand, in sight of all my foes,
　　Doth still my table spread;
My cup with blessing overflows,
　　His oil anoints my head.

The sure provisions of my God
　　Attend me, all my days;
Oh, may His house be mine abode,
　　And all my works be praise:
There would I find a settled rest,
　　While others go and come—
No more a stranger, or a guest,
　　But like a child at home.

　　　　　　　　　　　—Isaac Watts.

V

THE FULL TABLE

"Thou preparest a table before me in the presence of mine enemies; thou anointest my head with oil; my cup runneth over."

I do not think that any one can read this exquisite little Psalm with thought and attention without being conscious of a slight break at this verse five, or if not of a " break," of a change in atmosphere and colour and scenery. I am not suggesting that there is any change in the main theme. This little Psalm is a perfect unity, made such by the one note that throbs and thrills through it from the first sentence to the last—the note, viz., of a quiet and happy trust in God. Musicians, as my readers know, speak of the *motif* of a musical composition. A musical *motif* is a short theme or phrase, which becomes the subject of endless variations and upon which, as a foundation, an elaborate composition is built. But although the variations may be numerous, through them all the *motif* is continually to be heard, and it is the recurrence of that *motif* that gives unity and coherence to the whole. The *motif*, you may say, is the text upon which the rest of the music is but exposition and commentary. Now the *motif*, the theme, that goes singing through this Psalm is that of faith in the love and care of God. But at this verse five we come across a variation. Up to this point the Psalmist has illustrated the protecting care of God by means of the figure of a shepherd. At this point he substitutes for the shepherd the figure of a royal Host. The scenery changes from the open fields, the green pastures, the still waters, the dark gorges of the Bethlehem country, to the stately halls of some royal palace where the feast is spread.

"Thou preparest a table before me in the presence of mine enemies, thou anointest my head with oil, my cup runneth over." I am quite aware that all commentators do not take this view. There are some who maintain that the figure is still that of the shepherd and his sheep. When dusk falls, the shepherd takes his sheep to the greenest and most luscious pastures so that they may sleep full fed. And though through the gathering darkness the shapes of slinking wolves may be seen gliding hither and thither, under the sufficient protection of the shepherd the sheep eat in perfect safety. That interpretation may be made to fit in with the first sentence of the verse, but it seems almost impossible to interpret in any natural fashion the two last clauses, "thou anointest my head with oil, my cup runneth over," of a shepherd and his sheep. Those two clauses are redolent of the festal chamber. The provision of fragrant anointing oil was inseparably associated with festal occasions in the East. You remember how our Lord charged Simon the Pharisee with discourtesy for neglecting to provide it; while the full cup was the proof and evidence of the bounty of the host's hospitality. You remember again how it was the fear of the reproach of niggardly hospitality, as evidenced by the empty cup, that led directly to our Lord's first miracle at the wedding feast of Galilee. Altogether I do not hesitate to say that the figures of my text—the full table, the anointing cil, the mantling cup—interpreted naturally, suggest a feast—the bounteous provision of a royal Host—and nothing else.

So, in my exposition, I am going to take it for granted that the Psalmist has at this point changed his illustration. In this verse he pictures God as a princely Host. It is a familiar enough figure in the Bible. It was a figure which Jesus adopted in one, if not in two, of His most beautiful parables. God is the great Host who makes a feast for the wedding of His Son, and to that feast He issues His invitations broadcast. So ample is His provision that He bids His servants call in the poor and the lame and the halt and the blind that His house may be filled. He is a Host of such abounding hospitality that there is " enough

for each, enough for all, enough for evermore."
And while the idea of God as a bountiful host
is a familiar Bible idea, its introduction here
in no way breaks up the unity and symmetry of
this little Psalm. Dr. Davidson says that
" much is gained, even from the point of view
of art, by this additional figure to describe
God's goodness and man's ground of trust and
confidence. But whether the change of figure
enriches the little Psalm or not, at any rate, it in
no way impairs its unity. For the thought is
unchanged. David's spirit of trust in God per-
vades the whole Psalm. Mr. Stopford Brooke
says: " It enters into all its ideas and images.
It is this which harmonizes all its contrasts,
mellows all its changes, and unites into one
whole the quiet contemplation of the first
verses, the gloom of the fourth, the triumph of
the fifth and the combined retrospect and
prophecy of the last."

" Thou preparest a table before me in the
presence of mine enemies." I rather fancy that
we have here again a page from David's per-

sonal history. This is not to be written down as a bit of imagination or fancy, but it is just a transcript of the writer's own experience. There is a large element of autobiography in this little Psalm and there is autobiography in this sentence. David had spent a large portion of his life in the presence of his enemies. In the early years when he was a fugitive from the wrath of Saul he went in hourly danger of his life. And yet, looking back, he could see that God always " provided a table " for him. He had provided for the physical support of himself and his men—even though on occasion the holy bread had to be taken from off the altar in order to do it. And since he had been king, though wars had been so incessant that he had become a " man of blood," yet God had without lapse or failure provided for him and his people. He and they had lacked no good thing. And it was not of the provision of material food, physical support, that David thought merely. He had lived his life in presence of foes more terrible and deadly than the men who sought his life and his kingdom. He had lived in the presence of enemies who sought after his soul to destroy it. David was a man of like passions with ourselves; perhaps indeed a man of fiercer and more turbulent passions than most of us. There were raging, •tearing lusts in David's soul, and there were fierce temptations that perpetually set those lusts of his on fire. The very position he occupied—as monarch whose will was law—lent added power to his foes and made the fight for his own soul the harder. And the fight often went against him. The record of his failure is here in this book. His soul was amongst the lions again and again. But he never fell finally into their power. When he cried to God, there was always strength forthcoming to bring him off more than conqueror. And when he fell, there was ever mercy to restore him. God continually gave him the oil of joy for mourning, the garment of praise for the spirit of heaviness—so that, looking back and noting how God had furnished him with mercy and grace, enough for every emergency, whether of struggle or of failure, he sets this down as his great and happy experience— " Thou preparest a table before me in the presence of mine enemies; thou anointest my head with oil, my cup runneth over."

Now the truth I want to emphasize is that David's experience may be ours, too. God can do all this for us as well as for him. God does not change. His love does not falter and His power does not fail. If we are willing to commit ourselves to His keeping care, as did this Psalmist, our testimony, too, will be that He prepares a table before us in the presence of our enemies. The main ideas of the verse are those of provision for our needs and festive rejoicing. It may be that David had his physical needs in mind as he penned these words. And it is still true that in that respect God provides for us a full table. The yearly harvest is His gift. We sit down day by day to eat food of His providing. He gives us each day our daily bread. And with the memory of those days still fresh in our minds when Germany tried to cut off our food supplies, we can say humbly and gratefully in the words of the Psalmist, " Thou preparest a table before me in the presence of mine enemies." And if you remind me at this point that large tracts of Europe are short of food, that something like starvation stalks through certain parts of Europe, that there is unemployment and consequent need here at home, I answer " Yes." But the need and want and shortage are not because of any failure on God's part. The earth is there as rich and fruitful as ever it was, ready now as always to reward with bountiful harvests the industry of men, but if men persist in giving themselves to strife instead of to industry, and if by the ravages of war they turn into deserts what God meant to be fruitful fields, shortage and want are bound to ensue. The fault is not God's, it is ours. Let men turn their swords into ploughshares and their spears into pruning hooks; let them abjure war and give themselves to the pursuits of peace, and there will be no shortage. A teeming earth will demonstrate anew that God prepares a table for us. But it is not God's provision for his physical need that is chiefly in the Psalmist's mind, but His provision for the soul. And it is upon *that* provision I want to concentrate attention.

OUR ENEMIES

First of all, I want you to notice the picture of the moral situation which this verse gives us. We are " in the presence of our enemies." This is in accord with the teaching of the Bible from the first page to the last. Life, according to the Bible, is, from beginning to end, a conflict; it is a fight from which there is no discharge. It is not a barrack-square parade; it is a fierce campaign. Military figures abound in the Bible. And the military figures abound just because life is a struggle, a wrestle, a battle, an unending fight. I do not say that the fight continues equally hotly and fiercely at every stage. The battle ebbs and flows. Some fights

men definitely win and the particular foe
ceases to trouble them. There are men, for instance, who have won a decisive victory over
the drink habit. But beaten in one particular
section of the field, the foe may attack us in
another. If a man comes scatheless out of the
fight with the insurgent passions of youth, he
may fall victim to the cares of the world and
the deceitfulness of riches, which are the pe-
culiar peril of middle age. Always the fight
goes on. We are never allowed to put our
swords into the scabbard. Life ends with a
fight. The last enemy that must be faced and
conquered is death. This is the moral situation
in which we find ourselves, no matter what our
age or condition. We are in presence of enemies—or as one well-known hymn puts it,
"We are in the midst of foes."

These foes are many and various. To begin
with there are certain impulses and desires and
passions in ourselves which have to be held in
check or else they will sweep the soul into
destruction and perdition. I am not going to

discuss how we came by it. I am content now with noting the fact that we are born with a certain taint in the blood, a certain bias toward evil. "The flesh lusteth against the spirit," says St. Paul. We know it. The pull of the flesh, the tug of the lower nature is tremendous. But we know, too, that to yield is to degrade and coarsen and defile life. But the fight against these appetites that clamour for appeasement means agony and bloody sweat. And then in addition to the weaknesses and passions of our own nature, we live in a world which is full of incitements to evil. Our own hearts contain the gunpowder, the world applies the match. Our own hearts harbour the desire, the world affords the opportunity. The world —I mean the whole tone and temper and spirit of our present environment—is hostile to what is best and holiest. The world is enmity against God. This is not mere pulpit rhetoric. Everyone who takes life seriously and wants to live nobly knows that it means a constant fight to resist the pressure of the world in which we live, for to surrender to the pressure would mean the sacrifice of the soul. The very things the world loves and most ardently seeks may be fatal to the higher life. The soul may not only be drowned in destruction and perdition through youthful lusts; it may also be choked by the cares of the world and the deceitfulness of riches.

And then according to the testimony of this Old Book, in addition to the passions of our own nature, and the pressure of the world, we have to contend against a whole hierarchy of evil spirits. There is an organized kingdom of evil with its prince, who has subordinate evil spirits at his command. I know that the idea of evil spirits and a personal devil is scouted by a great many people as a pure superstition. But I see no more reason to doubt the existence of discarnate evil beings than I do to doubt the existence of angels; and there are facts in life, in the personal spiritual life of people which are hard to account for except on the supposition that there are evil spirits ceaselessly busy suggesting unholy thoughts and desires—luring, tempting, goading men into sin. At any rate these evil spiritual forces were real enough to the New Testament writers. You remember Paul's words, " We wrestle not against flesh and blood, but against the principalities, against the powers, against the world rulers of this darkness, against the spiritual hosts of wickedness in the heavenly places." That is the moral situation—" We are in the midst of foes."

THE PREPARED TABLE

Now the joyful assurance of this verse is that in the very presence of these enemies of ours there is always the prepared table. In the midst of encompassing foes there is support and security. I like the realism and frankness of the Bible. There is no promise here that our foes shall vanish and disappear—the promise is that such strength and support will be provided for us that we shall not need to fear them. I do not know that evil desire and passion and appetite ever completely die out of the soul. They may perhaps get less turbulent and insurgent with the passage of the years. But they still remain. That was one of the things that never ceased to perplex John Bunyan—the presence of sin in the regenerate. But though the evil emotions and desires remain, if we are in the keeping of God they remain only to be checked and beaten down if they seek to assert themselves. Even in face of these domestic foes, God keeps us in security. He prepares our table for us in the presence of our enemies. So long as we live in the world we shall be exposed to the pressure of the world—to its temptations to barter eternal things for temporal things, and spiritual blessing for material wealth. But though in the world we need not be of it, and though exposed to its temptation we need not yield to it; temptation need not develop into sin. In the keeping of God we are secure against its seductions. He strengthens us to rise superior to all its blandishments. We may have the world beneath our feet. You remember how that as

Christian went on his way towards the Porter's Lodge, he espied two lions on the road. At the sight of them he was for the moment terrified and half minded to turn back. But he plucked up heart and pressed forward, keeping to the middle of the road. And he found that the lions could not reach him. They roared at him but they could do him no harm, for they were chained. That is it exactly. The hostile evil world is still there. But if we are kept by God, it cannot hurt us. He supplies us with strength to rise above all its temptations. He provides a table before us, in the presence of our enemies.

And what of those evil principalities and powers of which St. Paul speaks? Well, even against their attacks we are kept in security. We have sufficient grace imparted to us to put the world, the flesh and the devil beneath our feet. There is a tremendous contrast between the seventh and eighth chapters of St. Paul's epistle to the Romans. In the seventh his soul is among the lions. You can hear the wild beasts snap and snarl. "The good that I would, I do not; the evil that I would not, that I practise; wretched man that I am; who shall deliver me from this dead body." But chapter eight breathes an atmosphere of serenity and joy. The enemies are still there, but he is no longer afraid of them. "Neither life nor death nor principalities nor powers, nor height nor depth (all these spiritual foes of whom Paul stood in such dread) nor things present, nor things to come shall be able to separate us from the love of God which is in Christ Jesus our Lord." What intervened between chapter seven and chapter eight? Paul's experience of the grace of God in Christ. That made him safe. Paul looks his old foes in the face and triumphs over them. God prepared a table before him in the presence of his enemies.

And so He will do for us if we commit ourselves to His keeping. We are in the midst of foes, but they shall not be able to hurt us. They can only gnash their teeth in helpless and impotent rage. "Tho' the wolves may ravin, none can do us harm." Over our own passions and the world's temptations and the devil's incitements we can, through the strength which God supplies, come off victorious. Be not, therefore, affrighted of your adversaries. God will keep you in security and peace. " Thou preparest a table before me in the presence of mine enemies."

The " prepared table " I have been suggesting stands for the strength which God supplies to all who trust Him, and which enables them to put the world, the flesh and the devil beneath their feet. But what about those who have been beaten down by their own lusts and passions, who have been beguiled by the world and taken captive by the devil at his will? I have been saying there is strength to be had enough to enable us to master and conquer temptation, but what about those who have fallen into sin? There is a full table for the tempted saint, is there a table provided for the guilty sinner? Yes, there is. Indeed, there would not be much hope for any one of us if there weren't. For we have all sinned and come short of the glory of God. We are all lost and guilty and undone.

But for us, too, God has provided a table. He provided one for David. For David fell low and sinned shamefully. But God provided a table for him—a table of mercy and free forgiveness. And He provides the same table for fallen and sinful men still. " Come and let us return unto the Lord and He will have mercy upon us, and to our God, for He will abundantly pardon.

This table was not provided without cost. God gave His Son, His only Son, in order to provide this table of mercy and free forgiveness. He gave Him to pain and shame and death. But the result is a table is provided for sinful men. Mercy and pardon and peace are now proffered to all. *Thou* providest a table. No one else could have provided *this* table. We could never have earned forgiveness. We could never have merited mercy. Only God, by the sacrifice of His Son, could provide this table.

> " There was none other good enough,
>   To pay the price of sin,
> He only could unlock the gate
>   Of heaven and let us in."

But the table is now provided. The Lord's body has been broken and His blood has been shed, and now mercy and pardon are provided for us all. "Thou preparest a table before me in the presence of mine enemies." And the guilty soul has its enemies. Law is its enemy, death is its enemy, the judgment is its enemy. But in face of God's provided mercy, law and death and judgment are all powerless to hurt. Law has no claim. "There is now no condemnation to them that are in Christ Jesus." Death has no terror.

> "There is no death for me to fear,
> Since Christ my Lord hath died."

And judgment has no fear. "We have boldnesss in the day of judgment." Mercy triumphs over judgment. The love of God comes between a man and his sins. Here is the Gospel for every sin-burdened soul. God has mercy for every guilty soul. Christ has made propitiation for the sins of the world. And once we have partaken of that mercy, law and death and judgment cease to terrify and appal. " Thou preparest a table before me, in the presence of mine enemies."

" Thou anointest my head with oil, my cup runneth over."

If the prepared table stands for God's provision for our need, the fragrant oil and the mantling and overflowing cup stands for the joyfulness of the Christian life. There can be no joy as long as life is dubious, checkered, broken. There can be no joy so long as we are haunted by fears. There can be no real happiness so long as we are burdened by sin. But when once life becomes strong and victorious, once our sins have been taken away and our fears removed joy and song come stealing in. Life becomes a high festival. Joy always comes in the train of deliverance. " Thou anointest my head with oil, my cup runneth over." There is a certain magnificence about God's providing! There is nothing skimpy or niggardly about it. He never confines Himself to bare necessaries.

When He made a world, He didn't make it on utilitarian principles. He made it gay with flowers, glorious with the crimsons of sunsets and dawns, musical with the whispers of the winds and the caroling of the birds. He made it full of splendour and of joy, beauty and light. "His paths," says the Psalmist, "drop fatness." There is a certain lavishness, a certain extravagance, a certain overflow in the goodness of God. And so it is in the highest realm. When the youngest son came back it was bare sustenance he asked for—life on any terms. But his father gave him a ring for his hands and shoes for his feet; he put on him the best robe, and there was music and dancing. He gave him more than sustenance; he gave him the joy of the son's place. And God does more than prepare a table. He does more than provide support and security. He gives us gladness. He does more than pardon, He gives us joy.

VI

GOODNESS AND MERCY

The Lord's my Shepherd, I'll not want
  He makes me down to lie
In pastures green, He leadeth me
  The quiet waters by.

My soul he doth restore again;
  And me to walk doth make
Within the paths of righteousness,
  Ev'n for His own name's sake.

Yea, though I walk in death's dark vale,
  Yet will I fear none ill;
For Thou art with me, and Thy rod
  And staff me comfort still.

My table Thou has furnish'd
  In presence of my foes;
My head Thou dost with oil anoint,
  And my cup overflows.

Goodness and mercy all my life
  Shall surely follow me;
And in God's house for evermore
  My dwelling-place shall be.

               —Scottish Psalter 1650.

VI

GOODNESS AND MERCY

"Surely goodness and mercy shall follow me all the days of my life, and I will dwell in the house of the Lord forever."

I have failed altogether in my exposition of this Psalm if I have not made you feel that from the first sentence to the last it is just a happy, sunny song of confidence and trust. I am not at all sure that this little Psalm does not represent the high water mark of faith so far as the Old Testament is concerned. " Perhaps," says Bishop Perowne in his commentary, " there is no Psalm in which the absence of all doubt, misgiving, fear, and anxiety is so remarkable." From one point of view, this Book of Psalms, this great book of devotion, may be described as the expression of the faith of elect and believing souls. But in it we see faith in all sorts of moods, in all sorts of attitudes, in all sorts of conditions and circumstances. In some Psalms we see faith fighting for its life; faith 'struggling with unfaith, faith almost overwhelmed and beaten to the ground, faith " scarcely saved "; but in this Psalm we see faith victorious, faith serene and untroubled. Some Psalms are cries from the depths; some are broken by sobs and moans; but this Psalm is like a lark's song on a spring morning. The Psalmist sings all the way through. He sings not only when he is being led into green pastures and by still waters, and when he is being guided along paths of righteousness, but he sings also when he passes through valleys of deep gloom. Nothing can disturb his faith; nothing can quench his joy. He is sure of the care and love of God, and so he rejoices always. He sings under all skies and in all circumstances. But the song reaches its climax, its glorious fortissimo, in this verse with which the Psalm closes. " Surely, goodness and mercy shall follow me all the days of my life and I will dwell in the house of the Lord forever."

You may search literature through and you will not discover a more jubilant, triumphant, exultant expression of happy confidence than that. "Surely!" That is a fine note to strike at the commencement. He starts off with a "loud, triumphant chord." This is no guess or "perhaps"—this great optimism of this verse. It is a solid certainty verified by the Psalmist's own experience. There is something peculiarly comforting in the very word— especially to such an age as ours. For the characteristic of our age is that we are not very sure about anything. Our age, Dr. van Dyke has said, is an age of doubt whose fitting crest would be an interrogation mark and its appropriate motto "Query." We question of life and death and sin. We faintly trust. We dimly see. "Faith and unfaith can ne'er be equal powers," says Tennyson. Well, perhaps not. But there may be little between them on the balance. And to a vague, wavering, dubious age like ours there is something exhilirating and bracing about speech that begins

like this. " Surely "—especially when the
" surely " introduces so glorious an affirmation
as this. But though the word " surely " strikes
so brave a note I am not at all certain that the
word David used does not really strike a note
braver still. This is the grammatical comment
Dr. Davidson makes upon the word: " The
opening word is sometimes affirmative, as in the
Revised Version text ' surely '; it is sometimes
restrictive, as in the Revised Version margin
' only.' Now oftentimes the revisers retained
a word in the text because it had been made
sacred by long usage, while they relegated the
more accurate translation to the margin. They
seem to have done so here. ' Only ' is the better translation of the word David used. And
while ' surely ' is a grand opening to this verse,
' only ' is grander still. ' Only ' goodness and
mercy shall follow me all the days of my life."

What a height this is to which the Psalmist's faith has risen! In the previous verse he
has spoken of " the presence " of his enemies.
All through the first four verses in which he

speaks of God as a shepherd there rises the thought of the wild beasts—the wolf and the lion—ready to snatch at the sheep. But by this verse, the snarl of the wolf has died away, and all his enemies have disappeared. Trouble, pain, loss, temptation, sin—they have almost ceased to exist for him. He is conscious only of the love and care of God. They fill his world for him. " Surely goodness and mercy shall follow me all the days of my life." You are most of you acquainted with Thompson's *Hound of Heaven*. The Hound of Heaven in that poem is just the seeking and redeeming love of God that pursues the sinner all down the years and through all the lands of sin and shame into which he may wander, intent upon rescuing and saving him. The sinner seeks to escape, but his one hope is that the Hound of Heaven pursues him without weariness—that love of God which will not let him go. David here too sings of the Hound of Heaven. Only he does not seek to escape it. He rejoices in that unwearied love. He exults in the thought that every day and all the day he is pursued, shadowed, attended by God's care and love. "Only goodness and mercy shall follow me all the days of my life."

On what does the Psalmist base this mighty but daring optimism of his? In a word, on the character of God as he himself has experienced it, on the character of God as shepherd and host, as shepherd guiding him along right ways and protecting him against all foes, and as host providing royally and lavishly for all his needs. David had found God to be all that to him in the course of his career, and basing himself on what he himself had known of the love of God, he knows that only goodness and mercy can follow him. I said in my study of the first verse of this Psalm that this was not a song of David's youth, but of David's age. It was not composed when he was a lad watching his father's sheep in the fields of Bethlehem; it was composed when he was a man, an old man, after passing through all those vicissitudes and all those tremendous personal experiences of which the Bible pages tell the story. And the assurance of the text is all the more convincing on that account. This is not the gay and irresponsible optimism of youth. Youth is apt to paint everything in rose colour. Youth, untouched by serious trouble, is ready enough to say " all's well with the world." But this is not the effervescence of youth. It is the sober judgment of age. David had had his share of trial and trouble—deep, poignant, tragic. But through all the changes of his career he had found God to be both shepherd and host—he had found God protected him and provided for him. He had found God's kindness and love never failed. And it is on the character of God as he had discovered it in his own experience that he bases himself when he gives utterance to this mighty optimism. " Surely goodness and mercy shall follow me all the days of my life."

We know more about the character of God than David did. He only knew God as revealed in his own experience; we know God as revealed in Jesus Christ, and especially in

Christ's cross. We know love is God's nature —love so deep and strong that it made the last and utmost sacrifice. Basing ourselves on the character of God as revealed in Christ, we can with even more assurance than the Psalmist dare to hold this splendid faith. With our God and Father at the helm we can be sure that only goodness and mercy will follow us all the days of our life; or, as the Christian Apostle puts it in slightly varying phrase, that all things must work together for good to them that love God.

THE REAR GUARD

Now, coming to look at the words more closely, I want you to notice that there is in the soaring assurance of this sentence an advance in thought over all that has gone before. All through the little Psalm breathes confidence and trust. In the first verse David declares that because the Lord is his Shepherd, " he shall not want." For the same reason he declares in the fourth verse that he " will fear no evil." In those two verses, as Dr. Maclaren says, the Psalmist's trust simply refused to yield to fear while keenly conscious of evil which might warrant it; but here he has risen higher and the alchemy of his happy faith and experience has converted evil into something fairer. The two former assurances, wonderful though they are, are negative. "I shall not want. . . . I will fear no evil." This is positive. "Only goodness and mercy shall follow me all the days of my life." David's assurance here is not simply that his life will be protected from harm, but that it will be enriched and blessed by the love and care of God.

And perhaps the reason for this advance in thought, this climax of faith, is this: that David became more conscious of his protectors than of his foes. I think his foes loom most largely before his vision in the previous verses, but his protectors fill the field here. "Only goodness and mercy shall follow me all the days of my life." He sees goodness and mercy like two bright-faced angels walking behind him as his rear guard. "Goodness" is the bounty that provides for need; "mercy" is the love that bestows more than is deserved. And as the Psalmist views his life he sees it attended by goodness and mercy as two guardian angels. And in view of these two mighty protectors, his foes cease to count; they vanish from his field of vision. "*Only* goodness and mercy shall follow me." I mentioned in the last chapter that amongst the enemies we have to face there are certain spiritual foes—"the principalities and powers, the world rulers of this darkness, the spiritual hosts of wickedness in the heavenly places," of whom St. Paul speaks. They make a terrible list of foes. But we need not cower in face of them. For if we have spiritual foes we have also spiritual helpers and defenders. "The angel of the Lord encampeth round about them that fear Him, and delivereth them." And for our own courage and good hope we need to remember these unseen helpers. "Open his eyes, Lord, that he may see," was Elisha's prayer for his servant who had fallen into a panic when he saw Dothan invested by Syrians, and who had jumped to the conclusion that into their hands both he and his master were bound to fall. And God heard the prayer and opened the servant's eyes and he saw the mountain was full of horses and chariots of fire " round about Elisha." The helpers were more mighty and more numerous than the foes. And that was what brought to David the glorious and victorious certitude that beats through this closing verse—he saw goodness and mercy following him. " *Only* goodness and mercy," for at sight of these mighty helpers all his enemies seemed to have slunk away.

" Only goodness and mercy shall follow me." I wonder whether there is significance in that word " *follow* " ? I fancy somehow that David was more afraid of what lay behind him than of what lay in front of him. What lay in front of him? The valley of the shadow of death. But he feared no evil there; he was sure God's rod and staff would be with him for his comfort. What lay behind? A black record of sin and shame. I need not recall it. The ugly story is familiar enough. Murder and adultery were both in David's personal record. And for the tragedies that took place in the circle of his family David is not to be wholly absolved from blame. That past contained bitter memories for David. And what he was most afraid of was the remorse and condemnation that past entailed and perhaps also a recrudescence of those evil passions and habits which the practice of that past had fostered. David was afraid of his past. He feared the pains and penalties of his own sin. But when he looked back it was not the pursuing shapes of his own follies and sins he saw; he saw the angels of goodness and mercy attending his steps. Between him and his pursuing sins came God in all His love and grace. " Surely goodness and mercy shall follow me all the days of my life." And there is rich and rare comfort in this, not only for David, but also for us. Our most deadly danger comes from be-

hind. Rear guard attacks in war are the most
deadly of all attacks. How destructive and
terrible they may be we may learn from the
tragic story of Napoleon's retreat from Mos-
cow. The finest army in the world was there
practically destroyed by the ceaseless attacks of
a restless and merciless foe upon the flank and
rear of a retreating host. And it is from the
rear—from our own past—that our most
deadly peril arises. For our past is not past in
the sense that it is dead and buried. The dead
past never buries its dead. The past affects
the present. Yesterday lives on in today.
"Their works do follow them" is true not only
of the saints, but of the sinners, too. What
are the things that pursue us from the past and
menace our very life? I am going to mention
just two, though there are many others.

(1) There are the *evil habits* which the past
has formed. What we are today is the result
of all our yesterdays. In those yesterdays, perhaps, we lightly and unthinkingly formed some
foolish and sinful habit. We may have tried

to break it, perhaps in a measure we may have succeeded in breaking it. But we know the desire is still there. That is a terrible verse which says "His bones are full of the sins of his youth." But terrible though it is, it is terribly and tragically true. Many a man finds his own past the biggest obstacle in the way of living a clean and honourable life today. The reformed drunkard finds his most terrible foe is the drink thirst he himself has created. The converted profligate finds his most fearful struggles arise from an imagination polluted in its very grain by his own habitual filthiness of previous years. We, all of us, know something about this. The power of a sinful habit abides even after we may have broken with it. You remember that couplet in Tennyson's *Idylls* in which he makes one of his knights resolve to put away the evil uses of his life, but "they from all his life arise and say, Thou hast made us lords, and canst not put us down." And the fear is never quite absent lest these evil habits of ours, which we honestly want to put away, should reassert their power and make us bite the dust. But the gospel a little verse like this preaches is that "Goodness and mercy follow us." Between us and these evil habits of our past comes the goodness of God, and the goodness of God, as I said a moment ago, signifies the provision God makes over against our need. God's grace and enabling power defend us against the presence of our own evil past. He breaks the power of cancelled sin. He brings us off more than conquerors. God comes between us and our pursuing foes and rescues us from their attack. "Goodness and mercy follow us."

(2) And there are not only the evil habits which the past has formed, but there are the sins, black and shameful, of which the past contains the story. And those sins—the very memory of them—rise up in judgment to condemn us. We know quite well that for our sins God is justly displeased—that on account of these we deserve nothing but punishment and pain. They dog our steps—these unfor-

gotten sins of ours, and they clamour for our blood. But between us and those sins of ours that cry out against us and condemn us comes God. I look back and I can see not my sins. I see " goodness and mercy " following. " Goodness and *mercy!* " Between us and law and judgment and death, keeping them at bay, reducing them to impotence, banishing them indeed from sight, comes mercy. " As far as the East is from the West so far has God removed our transgressions from us." There is one word written large over the face of the Bible and that is *sin!* There is another word written in larger letters still and that is *forgiveness*. " Where sin abounds, grace doth much more abound."

We are safe against all pursuing foes—against the crippling power and the condemnation of our own past—because between us and them God comes. You remember that great verse in Isaiah in which the prophet says, " The Lord will go before you; the God of Israel will be your rearward." God in front and God behind. The same thought is in this Psalm, too. In verse three God is in front—" He guideth me in the paths of righteousness for His name's sake." In this verse six God is behind. " Surely goodness and mercy follow me." The Psalmist's life is encompassed by God. What wonder the joy was in his heart and the song upon his lips? For what harm could befall a life thus encompassed? The Psalmist was safe amid the unknown perils of the way because God was leading him along paths of righteousness; he was equally safe against all the foes that rose up out of his own past because " goodness and mercy followed him." " Surely goodness and mercy shall follow me *all the days of my life*." " All the days." The care of God never ceases! The vigilance of God never relaxes. His love never changes. Goodness and mercy shall follow us *all* our days; goodness to strengthen and mercy to forgive. The promise has been taken up and repeated by our Lord Himself. For Jesus is but the goodness and mercy of the Lord incarnate. And that is what the Incarnate Goodness and Mercy says: "Lo, I am with you all the days even to the end of the world." The days may differ from each other. Some may be sunny and others may be overcast; some may be stormy and others may be calm; but whatever the nature of the day Christ will be with us caring for us, and that means that "only goodness and mercy shall follow us all the days of our life."

THE HOUSE OF THE LORD

And now I turn for a moment to speak about the second clause of the verse. "And I shall dwell in the house of the Lord for ever." The triumphant assurance of this second sentence is the consequence of the great affirmation of the first. I do not know that David would have been so sure about "dwelling in the house of the Lord for ever" if he had not been sure that "goodness and mercy" were following him. If goodness and mercy had not been following him David's sins and passions might have got the better of him; he might have wandered off into the far country and made his bed in hell. But seeing that " goodness and mercy " were following him, knowing that God's wisdom and love were attending to his guidance and protection, he was certain that he should dwell in the house of the Lord for ever. His confidence was based, not on his own strength at all, but on God's forgiving love and keeping care.

The commentators are not agreed as to what exactly David means by " dwelling in the house of the Lord for ever." When we read this little sentence we naturally and instinctively think of heaven and Perowne is loath to give up the idea that David may have had some anticipation of an everlasting sanctuary above. But we must beware of reading into David's words beliefs that belonged to a much later time. There is no direct allusion to a future life in the words " for ever," says Davidson, though he adds that neither is there any exclusion of the thought. Perhaps we had better say that when David talks about " dwelling in God's house for ever " he is thinking of uninterrupted fellowship and communion with God. " The house of the Lord " was the tabernacle, and later the temple. And it was the aspiration of many a pious Psalmist to abide there. But he wanted to abide there in order that the communion might be uninterrupted. That uninterrupted communion was the essential thing. And that was what David wanted, and that is what he was quite sure he should enjoy. " I shall dwell in the house of the Lord for ever." Dr. Maclaren says that " dwelling in the house of the Lord " in this sense was regarded as possible even while hands are engaged in ordinary duties and cares. David, even when occupied with the great affairs of kingship, might yet dwell in the Lord's house. The communion might continue unbroken. And perhaps he had a moment of high vision when the conviction was borne in upon his soul that such communion never *could* be broken. David, like the rest of the Jews, had no clear faith in a hereafter, but perhaps he felt that this blessed fellowship simply could not end; that it was bound to go on somewhere. That is one of the mighty and most irrefragable arguments for immortality. God will never surrender His friends. God does not call men into friendship with Himself to let that friendship perish in a few years. God is faithful—faithful to His friends—and that friendship is bound to continue some other where. And perhaps David, in a moment of insight, had it flashed in upon him that not even death could interrupt his fellowship with God. He would for ever remain in some "house of the Lord." It was a faith like Whittier's:

> "I know not where His islands lift,
>   Their fronded palms in air.
> I only know I cannot drift
>   Beyond His love and care."

"I shall dwell in the house of the Lord for ever."

But living, as we do, in the enjoyment of the

light of Christ we can use these words with a fulness of meaning impossible to David. "We can dwell in the house of the Lord" all the days we sojourn on this earth. Jesus, when about his carpenter's work, was still in the Father's house and about His Father's business. And we, too, attended as we are by goodness and mercy, cared for as we are by the Father's love, may live in heaven even while our business is on earth; we may hold high and blessed fellowship with God even while pursuing our ordinary avocations; we may work in shop or office and yet sit down in the heavenly places with Christ Jesus. And the high and holy fellowship thus established shall never be broken. We shall dwell in the house of the Lord "for ever." For in the Father's house there are many mansions. We live in an outlying mansion now. What happens at death is that we are called into another mansion "fairer than this we leave and lovelier," where the fellowship becomes closer and more intimate still. When we depart it is to be with Christ, which is far better. Those who have fallen asleep in Christ have not perished, but being absent from the body are at home with the Lord. The Lord spreads a table before us here, in the presence of our enemies. And He has a supper waiting for us up yonder—with no glimpse of a foe to mar our peace—the marriage supper of the Lamb, and from that supper—and those halls all jubilant with song, we shall no more go out. We shall " dwell in the house of the Lord for ever."

On that note, that happy and exultant note, this little Psalm ends. Those who put themselves in the care and keeping of God shall not lack for guidance, protection, provision, as they journey through life. And when life draws to its close, God's love does not fail. With God the best is always still to be. He keeps the good wine always to the last. For after seeing us safely through the valley He brings us to the house of the Lord, where faith shall become sight and dream shall become deed, and hope shall become fruition, and where every desire of the soul shall be satisfied. And in that house of the Lord we shall dwell for ever.

" So when my latest breath,
    Shall rend the veil in twain;
By death I shall escape from death
    And life eternal gain:
Knowing as I am known,
    How shall I love that word
And oft repeat before the throne:
    ' Forever with the Lord.' "